"Vassilis Saroglou wrote a wonderful book. *The Psychology of Religion* is a delicately crafted snapshot of what recent research in this field has to teach us. It presents a clear, compelling, and skillfully accurate account of the fundamental questions and the respective research conclusions. Scientific psychology seldom yields one-sided answers to important questions. This book is meticulously constructed with no bias or agenda – the best in scholarship, as we have come to expect from one of the most respected researchers in this area in this generation. Very highly recommended."

— **Raymond F. Paloutzian**, Editor of the *International Journal for the Psychology of Religion*, 1998–2016

"Although the psychological study of religion is more than a century old, it has only flourished vigorously in the last two decades. Vassilis Saroglou offers a master class in how to navigate this rich and variegated body of research. His overview is measured, balanced, and eminently readable. For readers who seek thoughtful, empirically-based answers to basic questions about the psychological antecedents and consequences of religion – as well as its likely future – this book should be a priority. It will be a trustworthy guide for experts and novices alike."

— **Paul Harris**, Harvard University

"This is a remarkable treatise of religion and religiosity from multiple approaches and psychological disciplines, and from an international, culture-sensitive perspective. The book provides a balanced approach of religiosity, fundamentalism, non-religious spirituality, and atheism. It is written in an accessible and engaging style by one of the foremost authorities on the subject. Highly recommended!"

— **Constantine Sedikides**, Professor of Social and Personality Psychology, University of Southampton

THE PSYCHOLOGY
OF RELIGION

Does religion positively affect well-being? What leads to fundamentalism? Do religious beliefs make us more moral?

The Psychology of Religion explores the often contradictory ideas people have about religion and religious faiths, spirituality, fundamentalism, and atheism. The book examines whether we choose to be religious, or whether it is down to factors such as genes, environment, personality, cognition, and emotion. It analyses religion's effects on morality, health, and social behavior and asks whether religion will survive in our modern society.

Offering a balanced view, The Psychology of Religion shows that both religiosity and atheism have their own psychological costs and benefits, with some of them becoming more salient in certain environments.

Vassilis Saroglou is Professor of Psychology at the University of Louvain, Belgium. He has conducted extensive research on religion from the perspective of social, personality, cross-cultural, moral, and emotion psychology.

THE PSYCHOLOGY OF EVERYTHING

People are fascinated by psychology, and what makes humans tick. Why do we think and behave the way we do? We've all met armchair psychologists claiming to have the answers, and people that ask if psychologists can tell what they're thinking. The Psychology of Everything is a series of books which debunk the popular myths and pseudo-science surrounding some of life's biggest questions.

The series explores the hidden psychological factors that drive us, from our subconscious desires and aversions, to our natural social instincts. Absorbing, informative, and always intriguing, each book is written by an expert in the field, examining how research-based knowledge compares with popular wisdom, and showing how psychology can truly enrich our understanding of modern life.

Applying a psychological lens to an array of topics and contemporary concerns – from sex, to fashion, to conspiracy theories – The Psychology of Everything will make you look at everything in a new way.

Titles in the series:

For further information about this series please visit www.routledge textbooks.com/textbooks/thepsychologyofeverything/

THE
PSYCHOLOGY
OF RELIGION

VASSILIS SAROGLOU

Routledge
Taylor & Francis Group

LONDON AND NEW YORK

First published 2021
by Routledge
2 Park Square, Milton Park, Abingdon, Oxon OX14 4RN

and by Routledge
52 Vanderbilt Avenue, New York, NY 10017

Routledge is an imprint of the Taylor & Francis Group, an informa business

© 2021 Vassilis Saroglou

British Library Cataloguing-in-Publication Data
A catalogue record for this book is available from the British Library

Library of Congress Cataloging-in-Publication Data
A catalog record has been requested for this book

ISBN: 978-0-8153-6811-3 (hbk)
ISBN: 978-0-8153-6812-0 (pbk)
ISBN: 978-1-351-25596-7 (ebk)

Typeset in Joanna
by Apex CoVantage, LLC
Printed and bound by CPI Group (UK) Ltd, Croydon CR0 4YY

CONTENTS

1

CAN WE STUDY RELIGION
IN THE LAB?

Psychologists are expected to study all kinds of human thoughts, feelings, and behavior. Their job is to deepen our understanding of human nature in terms of what motivates people and what the individual and social implications of people's cognition, emotions, personality, values, and identities may be. They do this across all levels of analysis, from genetics and biology to the social and the cultural, through the intra-individual, the interpersonal, and the intergroup levels. Finally, they study behavior – of humans, but sometimes animals too – across the many domains of people's activity, be they universal, like sexuality, learning, or meaning-making, or varying importantly across individuals and groups, like interest and investment in art, sports, or tourism. Thus, psychologists can, and should, also study religion.

PSYCHOLOGY'S CURIOSITY FOR RELIGION

A TOPIC FOR OPEN-MINDED INDIVIDUALS

Not all people are enthusiastic about the idea of psychologically studying religion. This is particularly the case with two kinds of people: some very religious and some very antireligious individuals. On the one hand, very religious people often think that it is impossible or useless to study religion through psychological methods and theories. Fundamentalist groups sometimes even prohibit psychologist researchers from distributing anonymous surveys to their members. These people think that religion is too sacred an object to be studied by limited human minds – in technical words, they believe science is reductionist. This is somewhat true, but this is the job of every scientific discipline: to study its object from a certain, thus limited, perspective. However, knowing the psychological determinisms that explain why certain people tend to fall in love with some specific kinds of individuals and not others should not prevent these couples from perceiving and experiencing their love as a miracle. The same is true for the psychological explanations of religious faith or atheism.

On the other hand, some very antireligious individuals, including scholars, think that the psychological and social scientific study of religion is useless or uninteresting. For them, religion is irrational like all paranormal beliefs, outdated and reflecting a primitive stage of human development, uninteresting to be studied since the basics are already known – religion is a refuge for the weak – and, if anything, dangerous for individuals' well-being and development and for society's peace. As we will see across this book, on the basis of the existing psychological research, these opinions are either false or constitute problematic overstatements. Finally, probably because psychology was a very young science trying to establish its scientific status, psychologist scholars have sometimes been reluctant to study religion. Especially in the context of secularized West, several psychologists even had the feeling that religion is marginal or irrelevant for people's life.

RELIGION AS SHAPING (SOME) INDIVIDUALS' LIVES AND ALL CULTURES

Contrary, however, to these extreme positions of the very religious or the very antireligious, psychological interest in religion and the related domains of spirituality, fundamentalism, and irreligion/ atheism has been constant, from the very early thinkers like William James, Sigmund Freud, B. F. Skinner, or Erik Erikson till today. This interest led to many decades of psychological research, with empirical methodology being the key feature distinguishing psychology from the more philosophical approach to understanding human nature. Furthermore, in the last 15 years, there has been an explosion of psychological research on religion. This is very likely because of the obvious need to understand the impact of religion on individuals and groups within a globalized world marked by certain civilizational conflicts. It may also be due to the arrival of a new generation of psychologist scholars characterized by both strong intellectual curiosity and higher ideological neutrality compared to their predecessors.

Independently thus of whether each of us is a believer or a nonbeliever, to understand human nature and the world today, we need to depart from our Western ethnocentrism and realize first that, today, more than 70 percent of the world's population reports being affiliated with a religious tradition. Why does religion persist? Why does atheism seem to increase rather slowly, if at all? (Atheists' relative weight in the world population may even decrease in 50 years because of believers' higher fertility rate.[1]) Second, societies and cultures differ importantly with regard to religious attitudes and behavior. In a recent international study, Gerard Saucier and his colleagues from 33 countries found that the largest cultural differences between countries concern religion and related moral norms and family values.[2] How and why are religious differences interrelated with other, nonreligious, cultural differences?

Moreover, it is also striking that, beyond the fact that societies may be or become less or more religious, there always exists within societies, even the most secularized ones, considerable variability between people, i.e. between believers and nonbelievers, as well as between different ways of expressing one's own religiosity or atheism. Why do people differ so substantially in their attitudes toward religious faith? Obviously, the psychological characteristics of these people (e.g. strong need to belong) and the reactions of these characteristics in the face of specific situations and contexts (e.g. loneliness or social ostracism) should be good candidates to explain such differences between people within the same society and often within the same family.

An important final clarification is that to study religion, as psychologists, we do not need to accept or even argue that religiosity or spirituality is a universal and basic dimension of human existence and personality. Together with several other scholars in this field, I conceive religiosity or spirituality as one among many other individual differences that are not necessarily universal or basic. For instance, a sense of personal and collective identity, as well as a sense of self-esteem, are both basic and universal: even if people may differ on how much they have thought and worked on their identity or not, or on how strong or vulnerable their self-esteem is, lacking a sense of identity and disposing of weak self-esteem are unfortunate situations that impair well-being. This is not the case with religiosity or spirituality. Being highly religious or being an atheist simply constitute diverse ways in which people deal with existential questions, afterlife beliefs, and related moral issues. Each of these ways has its own costs and benefits. Religion is thus like art or sport. Some invest in and practice it a lot, some less, and some not at all. As psychologists, we need to understand why people differ and the psychological implications of these differences in individuals' lives.

THE MEANINGFUL VARIETY OF RELIGIOUS ASPECTS AND FORMS

What is "religion"? What is "spirituality"? How many forms of religiosity exist? I usually do not care much for definitions: I've come to suspect that providing many definitions is sometimes a rhetoric some people use to pretend that they are real scientists and that they know more than "the average" person. Nevertheless, I've also noticed over the years that the more we speak of intimate things, the more each of us has our own conceptions. So, it may be useful, at least for the clarity of communication, but also by respect for the existing scientific work, to present and comment on the most important notions we will deal with in this book.

BELIEVING, BONDING, BEHAVING, AND BELONGING

We can simply define religion as what people do – think, feel, and act – in reference to an entity, i.e. a person or an impersonal force, principle, or nature, that they perceive to be as transcending humans and the world. However, to distinguish religion from proximal but distinct human experiences implying some kind of reference to a transcendence, like, for instance, art, philosophy, or self-identifying with a nation, it is important to realize that we can talk about "religion" when four aspects, called for convenience the "big four Bs," are co-present. These are: (1) Believing, including specific unverified beliefs in relation to this transcendence; (2) Bonding, with the transcendence and co-religionists through public and/or private rituals involving emotions; (3) Behaving, in a way that conforms to some degree to a sacred authority; and (4) Belonging to a group legitimizing that authority. These four aspects of religion also correspond to four kinds of psychological needs or functions: cognitive, emotional, moral, and social.[3]

Thus, to fully psychologically understand religion and individual religiosity, one needs to understand the interplay between beliefs, rituals, values, and groupness, and cannot only study religion or religiosity as just a belief, a set of rituals, a system of values, or a group belonging. Indeed, it is the co-presence of the four dimensions that makes religion's role specific, possibly unique, in terms of the underlying processes – be it with positive or negative outcomes. For instance, religion promotes and shapes prosocial values through rituals and related emotions, moral codes and norms, sets of beliefs and narratives, and group belongingness. This is not necessarily the case, for instance, with secular ideologies, philosophical systems, law codes, or school-based moral and civic education.

These four dimensions are typically co-present. For instance, individuals who highly believe tend to also practice frequently; and religious doubt is a good predictor of stopping that practice. However, the four distinct aspects of religion also reflect *diversity* at both the individual and the collective levels. Individuals may be attached to religion, convert to faith, change religion, or de-convert and exit from religion, primarily for cognitive, emotional, moral, or social motives such as, respectively, search for meaning, emotional regulation needs, ideal of self-mastery, and the need to belong. Inversely, exiting from religion may occur after a person begins to find religious beliefs irrational, becomes unsatisfied with religious rituals, discovers a religious leader's moral hypocrisy, or is no longer proud of the community's history or present. Similarly, some religions, in some cultural contexts, may emphasize one or two of the four dimensions to a greater extent than the others. For example, as work by Adam Cohen and colleagues has shown, Jewish religiosity reflects a strong attachment to orthopraxy, norms, and identity, whereas Protestant religiosity emphasizes belief and faith.[4]

FROM SPIRITUALITY TO FUNDAMENTALISM: THE STRUCTURED DIVERSITY OF RELIGIOUS FORMS

Beyond the diversity in religious forms with respect to their emphasis on the cognitive, emotional, moral, or social dimensions, religious people can be different in other ways. A traditional distinction – though today criticized as having a predominantly Protestant flavor – has been between *intrinsic* religiosity and *extrinsic* religiosity. In the former, faith and religious values and goals constitute an end by themselves. In the second, individuals practice religion or self-define as religious as a means to achieve other, non-spiritual goals such as self-identifying with their ethnic community or achieving social advantages.[5]

Somehow similarly, one can distinguish between *devotional* religion and *coalitional* religion, i.e. respectively, intimately connecting with a transcendental reality versus connecting with a community and its norms and traditions. This distinction between the individual and the social dimensions of religious disposition is classic and underlines the fact that religion encompasses both a mystical-like, internal world-oriented dimension and an (in)group- and social world-oriented one as well. These two orientations may even conflict with each other within the religious person or the religious group. A typical example seen throughout history has been the smoldering conflict between mystics, monks, and prophets on one side, and religious leaders on the other.

Extending the previously mentioned distinction between the social and the individual facets of religion and religiosity, more recent research has distinguished between *traditional religiosity*, defined as the religious expressions within established religious groups, and *modern spirituality*, defined as the belief in a transcendence and the endorsement of related values (mainly the interconnectedness of all beings), but independently, if not outside of, the established religious groups and traditions. Overall, in surveys of samples from the general population, the two, religiosity and spirituality as opposed to the non-belief, are interrelated, and in traditional societies, the two may be almost interchangeable – in those societies, spirituality refers to the interior aspect of religious faith. But the further we move into modern secular societies, the more spirituality differs from religiosity, reflecting partly distinct personality tendencies and presenting partly different social outcomes.[6]

Another important source of diversity in religious forms concerns the way in which people deal with religious beliefs, texts, norms, rituals, authority, and group identity. Religious people vary greatly on a continuum from a flexible, symbolic, and open-minded style of interpreting and understanding this "material," to a rigid, literal, and closed-minded way of doing so. Note that I do not say here that religious people are either dogmatic or open-minded. In fact, the majority of religious believers are somewhere in the middle. If anything, they are motivated – at least across monotheistic cultural contexts – by an epistemic need for order, structure, and answers in their internal world – what may be a precursor to, but does not necessarily lead to, dogmatism.[7] Thus, it is the high and the low ends of the continuum that correspond to, respectively, the dogmatic and the flexible religious people.

At the high end of the continuum one can identify (1) religious *orthodoxy*, i.e. literal attachment to tradition, authority, and the normative; (2) religious moral *conservatism*, i.e. opposition to modern liberal values; (3) religious *fundamentalism*, i.e. dogmatic and exclusive religiosity, most often, but not necessarily, related to religious orthodoxy and conservatism; and (4) religious *radicalism*, i.e. active, militant, and sometimes violent fundamentalism. On the low end of the continuum one can find (5) the orientation of *religion-as-quest*, defined by Daniel Batson as the valuing of doubt and the openness to the possibility of changing one's own beliefs; and (6) a type of religiosity called *faith maturity*, an interesting construct denoting religious faith that has been progressively reworked and evolved with autonomy, but studied primarily in the context of Western Protestantism.[8]

It is important to note that there exists no clear evidence showing that religion itself makes people fundamentalists or high questers. Rather, it is people's specific personality traits, conservative or liberal social attitudes, and certain cognitive and emotional needs that push them, if they are or become religious, to orient themselves toward dogmatic or symbolic religious expressions. Nevertheless, this means that these people find "food" in religion to nourish and comfort their respective needs for rigidity or, to a lesser extent, flexibility.

A final distinction can be made between a religious orientation marked by positive emotionality and joy, and one marked by negative emotionality, anxiety, fear, or guilt. This distinction comes back to William James, the father of the American psychology of religion, who in 1902 developed the idea of two forms of religion: one of the "healthy minded," and the other, of the "sick soul."[9] Emotionally positive religion implies a positive, loving image of God as well as positive and adaptive ways to use religion to cope with life's difficulties. It is more typical of religiosity acquired through socialization. Emotionally negative religiosity implies, on the contrary, an authoritarian image of God as judging and punishing, as well as maladaptive religious means to cope with stress. It is often characteristic of people who have experienced rapid conversion (often called "dramatic") and/or join small, cultlike, religious movements.

HOW WE STUDY RELIGION IN THE LAB

Can we study religion "in the lab" given such a variety of forms of religiosity and diversity across the world between religious groups and traditions and their respective beliefs, practices, and norms? How is it still possible to speak of a psychology of "religion"? Similarly, is it reliable to do research and communicate scientific knowledge on the psychological determinants, characteristics, and consequences of "religiosity"? Scholars from the humanities, like anthropologists, historians, or biblical scientists, typically working on a precise spatial, historical, or textual "territory," often express such skepticism.

I think it is legitimate to use the singular when referring to the psychology of "religion" – and not of "religions" – and the psychology of "religiosity" – and not of the "varieties of religious experiences," to use the title of the seminal book of William James. Most cross-cultural psychologists today agree, based on the existing evidence, that one should avoid two extremes: excessive cultural relativism and naïve cultural universalism. I think this holds for religion too. First, it is highly striking and intellectually challenging that, despite the impressive number of several thousands of religions, churches, sects, and cults across the world, three-fourths of humanity identify with one of four major world religions. These are Hinduism (15 percent), Buddhism (7 percent), Christianity (31 percent), and Islam (24 percent).[10] Religions perhaps persist and flourish, and individuals find religious means to satisfy their psychological motives, as long as there is some continuity within traditions and similarity between traditions in the "top" proclaimed values such as compassion, self-mastery, and social cohesion – otherwise they should wonder whether they belong to a satanic cult.

Second, emerging accumulative research from the area of cross-cultural psychology of religion suggests that indeed, beyond notable differences in their detailed content, the beliefs, rituals, values, and ways of structuring the community across religions and cultures also exhibit impressive similarities in the psychological determinants, characteristics, and outcomes of religiosity. This is especially the case when inspecting the big picture: across and within societies, religionists greatly resemble each other when compared to nonbelievers.[11] To give only two examples: no religion, at least no successful religion that has survived and flourished, has promoted permissive sociosexuality or equal treatment of homosexuality and heterosexuality. In other words, the big or primary psychological distinction seems to be between religionists and nonbelievers. Subtler differences between religious forms or between religions also exist; but they do not overcome in size the "to be(lieve) or not to be(lieve)" division.

Thus, we can study the psychological characteristics of "religiosity" defined as a global positive versus negative disposition toward, and investment in, religion. We can do it especially if we are interested in the broad distinction in the general population between believers and nonbelievers. But we also can, and should, study the more specific and nuanced dimensions and forms of religiosity, especially if we are interested in religious believers or in "known" groups, i.e. members of certain religious groups. Similarly, we can study the effects and outcomes of "religion" on people's thoughts, feelings, and behavior. Again, this can refer to religion in general, with participants being stimulated by broad religious contexts and mindsets. For instance, people can be surveyed in front of a church (experimental condition) versus a town square (neutral condition) or be primed with a set of religious (again, experimental condition) versus nonreligious words (neutral). Alternatively, participants can be exposed to specific aspects of religious ideas and other elements. The latter can be done, for instance, by exposing participants to an image of a loving versus judging God, or by examining the influence of attending services at a charismatic versus mainstream religious community.

Thus, most, if not all of both classic and more recent methods of investigation across the major psychological fields (cognitive, neuroscientific, social, personality, clinical, developmental, and evolutionary psychology) can be, and have been, applied to the psychological study of religion. This includes for instance surveys or experiments in the lab, online, or in a natural environment, using (1) *self-reported* questionnaires or *ratings* by external observers or by familiar peers such as family members, friends, and colleagues; (2) *behavioral* measures, such as people's acts, decisions, facial expressions, or gestures, or more *implicit* measures, such as brain activity, physiological measures, and preferences or associations between concepts of which we are rather unaware; and (3) *factual data*, i.e. biographical data, genetic information, or actions performed and artifacts produced by individuals and groups, such as rituals, texts, images, or web content and messages.

These various kinds of measures may tap the religious tendencies under study or the hypothesized related psychological constructs. Also, in these studies, religion or religiosity may be conceptualized as (1) a *cause or predictor* (e.g. does religion make people more prosocial?), (2) an *outcome* (e.g. does guilt increase one's belief in God?), (3) a *correlate* of other psychological constructs (e.g. do orthodox religious people tend to dislike absurd humor?), or finally as (4) a *moderator* of other links (e.g. do religious believers react differently than nonbelievers when confronted with authority's unethical orders, like in the well-known Milgram experiment?). These kinds of studies may apply to individual cases, samples from the general population, or specific groups of any sort such as children, people with disabilities, cult members, jihad activists, prisoners, prototypical religious figures, political leaders, or survivors of a traumatic experience.

In addition to the typical research of psychology of religion that has been *cross-sectional* (all measures are taken at the same time) or *experimental* (a change, stimulation, or intervention is introduced to test its effects), we also now have nice *longitudinal* studies at our disposal, where people are followed for some years or even decades of their life. Moreover, we dispose today of focused *cross-cultural* studies, where specific cultural and/or religious groups within or across societies are compared, as well as many studies using *large international data* gathered from dozens of countries. These last studies allow for distinctions to be made between the influence of variables at the level of the individual, including one's personal religious characteristics, and the influence of variables at the collective – cultural group or societal – level. Those latter variables typically include cultural characteristics, socioeconomic indicators, as well as religious variables such as whether a country is religious or secularized, or whether the society's religious heritage is Protestant, Catholic, Orthodox, Muslim, Hindu, or Buddhist.[12]

BOOK CHAPTERS AND QUESTIONS

In the next chapters of this book, we will discover today's answers to the most important questions asked in relation to religion from a psychological point of view. I will focus on theory and scientific knowledge, based on empirical research that has a certain degree of solidity, i.e. studies that do not stand alone but replicate, and generalizability, i.e. the results are not specific to one particular sample in only one specific country and found by only one laboratory. Across the next five chapters, we will examine the cognitive, emotional, moral, and social dimensions of religion and religiosity, as well as the developmental, health-related, cultural, and evolutionary aspects. As specified in this introductory chapter, with "religion" we also include spirituality, fundamentalism, and (ir)religion/atheism. A presentation of select questions by chapter follows.

- Chapter 2: Why are there believers and nonbelievers? Is it all about education and socialization, or do psychological characteristics and possibly genetic predispositions also work to determine people's preferences on religious issues? Why do people convert to, or de-convert (exit) from, religion?
- Chapter 3: Is there a natural inclination for children in particular, but also adults, to believe in counterintuitive things like an omnipresent God, flying angels, and extraordinary miracles? Is

adolescence a sensitive period for disbelief and apostasy or for the maturation of spirituality and faith? Do late adults return to religion because of the fear of death?

- Chapter 4: Do religion's explicit values of compassion and love translate into people's behavior or are religious people moral hypocrites who only believe they are altruistic? Or does religiosity even fuel discrimination, exclusion, and violence against everyone who is different? Do nonbelievers tell white lies more easily than religious believers?

- Chapter 5: Is religion a source of psychopathology or is it rather good for our health and well-being? Or may atheism be better? Are the effects the same all over the world? Why do religious people dedicate significant amounts of their time to perform repetitively, weekly if not daily, the same private and public rituals, and for their entire life?

- Chapter 6: If the human species evolved by selection of some adaptive psychological mechanisms, has religion been a facilitator or an obstacle to this evolution? Will religion survive secularization, or will it disappear as societies and individuals become healthy, wealthy, and wise?

2

BELIEVERS AND ATHEISTS
WHAT MAKES THE DIFFERENCE?

In contemporary secular Western societies, it is generally accepted that we can criticize and even ridicule religions, but we cannot derogate ethnicity and ethnic groups. In many of these societies, the former is legally permitted, but the latter is punished. One possibility explaining this difference in treatment may be that we generally consider faith and religion – or unbelief – as being our choice; but we do not choose the ethnic group we belong to. However, are the two, religion and ethnicity, so different?

If faith and religion were exclusively our choice, then it is a bit ironic that, in societies where religion is normative, most people are religious; and in societies where secularism has become normative, nonbelievers are growing in numbers and sometimes exceed 50 percent. The religious map of the world indicates a nice correspondence between geography and predominance of a specific religion or denomination. If you are born in Pakistan, Greece, or the Czech Republic, there is a great likelihood that in your adulthood you will be, respectively, a Muslim (96 percent), Christian Orthodox (88 percent), or nonbeliever (60 percent).[1]

Thus, socialization is a key explanatory factor of religious belief and affiliation. Nevertheless, within societies, as well as within families, people also show important variability. Citizens, as well as siblings, who have received the same religious – or atheist – education in their family, may take very diverging pathways in their life span by either remaining a believer or nonbeliever (socialized religion or atheism), finding or intensifying faith (conversion), exiting from faith (de-conversion), or changing religious denomination (religious switching). Beyond socialization, people may experience the need for either continuation or change in self-concept, worldviews, ultimate goals, existential beliefs, and the religious tradition and community to which they belong. Such stability or change, with regard to (ir)religious socialization people have received, can be understood as resulting from two kinds of influences: personality and other individual differences one the one hand, and personal, unique to them, life experiences, on the other.

Interestingly, within societies across history, there have always been believers and nonbelievers. No side has succeeded to convince the other side. This chapter will provide detailed information on why individuals differ with regard to religiosity and why some people remain stable and others change. To do so, we will examine the interplay between environmental influences – mainly socialization and personal experiences – and psychological individual differences – mainly personality characteristics, genetic dispositions, and differences at the cognitive level. This will help us to also understand gender differences: across societies, women are more inclined to believe in God.

SOCIALIZATION

FAMILY, PEERS, AND SOCIETY

Parents, and often mothers more than fathers, play a key role in the intergenerational transmission of religious attitudes, beliefs, practice, affects, values, and identity. Beyond parents, to some extent, grandparents, in particular grandmothers, and sometimes siblings, have been found to play an additional role in shaping or boosting individual religiosity. The partial, not full, correspondence between a family's religious attitudes and those of their offspring is manifest not only in childhood and adolescence, but also in adulthood. Interestingly, some research indicates that what children think their parents believe influences their beliefs even more than the actual beliefs their parents hold. In addition to family members, other channels of religious socialization may of course be friends and other kinds of peers, as well as teachers, mentors, and religious and educational institutions.[2] It is, however, unclear whether the effects of these channels are unique or constitute indirect ways through which the parents' role is expressed – parents define to some extent their children's network of peers and educational and other institutions.

An important qualifier of the impact of family religiosity on the offspring's religiosity is the style of parenting. As Sam Hardy and colleagues have shown, the impact on young adults' religiosity seems to be stronger if parents favor autonomy and do not use rejection; and the impact on young adults' spirituality is stronger in families with greater warmth, structure, and autonomy support.[3] Another qualifier is *religious homogamy*, i.e. parents' similarity in religious attitudes and denomination. Family religious socialization may be more effective among children whose parents share the same religious faith and values. Interestingly, it has been found that, in interfaith families, children's religious affiliation is more similar to the mothers' than the fathers'.[4]

The previously mentioned trends emphasize how deeply people's religiosity is rooted to their family experience as children and adolescents. Those trends suggest that the psychological function of (socialized) religion may primarily be to foster connectedness with proximal others and continuity with our childhood world in order to ensure security, affection, structure, and feelings of wholeness. The mother's preponderant role may simply be due to the fact that women are more religious. Thus, mothers are more concerned with their children's religious education. It may also result from the fact that mothers have traditionally been stronger vectors of security, warmth, and attachment. Beyond subtle differences between fathers and mothers, it is evident that children grow up in families that constitute communities with a pro-religious, nonreligious, or antireligious microclimate. There is in fact strong *assortative mating*, i.e. matching between future parents on high versus low religiosity, as well as on conservative versus liberal values, while at the same time parents may resemble each other only slightly, or not at all, in personality traits.[5]

CULTURAL FACTORS: SECULARISM AND MINORITY RELIGION

Inversely symmetrical to religious socialization, *irreligious* (family) socialization also plays a key role in predicting adult irreligion. Moreover, as the number of young nonbelievers becoming parents is increasing, their role in socializing their children as nonreligious becomes clearer. Consequently, the proportion of socialized nonbelievers is increasing today.[6] It is early to have a clear picture on how socialized nonbelievers differ psychologically from disaffiliated nonbelievers, but initial evidence suggests that the de-converted are midway between socialized believers and socialized nonbelievers.[7]

Is religious socialization an effect of family or, rather, the broader social context? International data from numerous countries suggest that, in traditionally religious societies, parents' religiosity, though important, matters less than in secular countries. Moreover, societies with high income inequality, which are typically religious, provide a favorable context for broad religious socialization, even if individuals only receive little religious socialization within the family. In relatively secular nations, family religiosity strongly shapes children's religious beliefs, while the influence of the national religious context is small.[8]

The role of parents' religiosity becomes even more salient when religion has a minority status, in the context of a state's hostile policies against religion (e.g. in ex-socialist countries) or in the context of immigration. Studies among second-generation Muslim immigrants in Europe show that attachment to the heritage culture boosts religious intergenerational transmission; and family religious socialization, in particularly religious practices at home during childhood, has the strongest impact on the preservation of religious practices among young adults, whereas external socialization sources (friends, schooling) have little or no impact. Similar findings hold for second-generation Jewish immigrants in the US, indicating that the previously mentioned trends are not confined to the context of European Islam.

Nevertheless, there is a difference worth mentioning. Whereas first-generation immigrants generally tend to follow the global pattern of some religious decline due to secularization, later-generation Muslim immigrants in Europe are found in some studies to become more religious than their parents.[9] This probably results from a need for *optimal distinctiveness* from the native majority and a need to strengthen collective self-esteem in the context of perceived discrimination.

INDIVIDUAL CHARACTERISTICS (OR DISPOSITIONS)

Socialization is the most important factor explaining future adult religiosity, but not the only one. People with similar religious socialization turn out to differ considerably in their later religious attitudes. First, this is because even when similarly socialized, people differ with respect to several *psychological characteristics*, i.e. personality traits, cognition, and values. These traits render some individuals better predisposed to faith – to remain or become religious. Others are more inclined to be, remain, or become irreligious. Second, specific kinds of *life events* constitute critical personal experiences for self-transformation and change regarding existential, moral, and religious preferences. Next, we will examine these influences in detail.

What are the personality characteristics of religious people? Atheists often consider religious believers as being (1) emotionally unstable, weak, and vulnerable; (2) irrational and eager to endorse paranormal beliefs; and (3) dogmatic and inflexible. However, empirical research shows that the previously mentioned perceptions are either inaccurate or constitute excessive overgeneralizations. In fact, they correspond to very specific forms of religion or believing and do not reflect the psychological characteristics of the average religious believer and practitioner. More importantly, it is actually other personality traits that constitute the core psychological characteristics of common religiosity.

PERSONALITY TRAITS AND RELIGIOSITY

Religious people actually tend to be characterized by the combination of two broad personality tendencies called, in the current dominant Big Five model of personality, *agreeableness* and *conscientiousness*, and by a strong endorsement of the corresponding values of benevolence and conservation of personal and social order. To use a term from an older personality model (Eysenck's), religious people typically tend to be *low in psychoticism*, which is the cold, distant, uncontrolled, and antisocial dimension of personality.[10]

These broad tendencies imply thoughts, feelings, motives, values, and behaviors that denote, first, a personal disposition toward quality in interpersonal relationships, mostly with proximal others, what translates into trust, honesty, empathy, readiness to forgive, and compassion. Second, they denote search for order and stability at the intra-individual level (self-control, low impulsivity, industriousness), the interpersonal level (commitment, reciprocity), and the societal level (social cohesion, traditionalism, conformity).

If we focus on the other three out of the Big Five personality dimensions, common religiosity, overall, is not necessarily characterized by *emotional stability* or instability, *extraversion* or introversion, or *openness to experience* or closed-mindedness – only specific religious forms are. Similarly, though historically religions may have been developed as cultural tools to deal with the enigma of afterlife by promising literal or symbolic immortality, research does not confirm the idea that individuals who are more anxious about their death are necessarily more attracted to religion.

Note that the differences of believers compared to nonbelievers in personality traits are not big in size. They reflect, respectively, a

57–60 percent versus 43–40 percent likelihood to be agreeable or conscientious. However, it is the quasi-universality of these tendencies that is striking. The prosocial orientation of religionists' personality has been found across cultures, world religions, forms of religiosity, genders, ages, and historical periods. Similarly, their orientation toward order and stability seems to be very broadly present, at least across most monotheistic religious and cultural contexts.

One could suspect that these two tendencies simply reflect the need to get along with and please others and to conform with societal expectations. Research indeed confirms that religious people tend to appear to others and to themselves as good. However, research has also confirmed that the agreeable and conscientious tendencies of religionists really exist, beyond these *social desirability* biases, and have real-life consequences. For instance, as we will see in Chapter 4, religious people express their prosocial tendencies in the fields of study they chose and the humor styles they use. They also tend to be characterized not necessarily by the epistemic motivation for curiosity – which would reflect openness to experience, but rather the epistemic *need for closure*, denoting conscientiousness, i.e. the need for order, structure, and answers in the internal and external world.

Furthermore, longitudinal studies confirm the idea that people who are agreeable and conscientious at an earlier age, or experience increases in their agreeableness and conscientiousness as they age, tend, years and decades later, to be religious or experience increased religiosity. Thus, religiously socialized people who are agreeable and conscientious are more inclined, for motives related to family harmony and personal and social stability, to continue and preserve traditions, worldviews, existential ideology, and related values and practices of the family and the broader environment. Alternatively, people who have not been socialized as religious may, especially when they experience life events threatening the self (see next), turn to religious faith and practice more easily if they are agreeable and conscientious. Because of the very specific aspects of religious beliefs (e.g. God is loving and judging), rituals (e.g. celebrating forgiveness or reciprocity), norms (e.g. the golden rule), and communities (e.g.

social support and control), religions seem to attract individuals who are highly motivated by affection, meaning, and order, especially in difficult times.

Intriguingly at first glance, studies from behavioral genetics show heritability influences on religiosity versus irreligion. Though the influences on religiosity coming from the shared, common, environment (e.g. same family education) are preponderant, genetic influences can explain an important part of the variance. As for personality traits, the genetic influences on religiosity become clearer in early adulthood, probably because this is the age in which young adults maximize their autonomy with regard to family and school, and their individuality emerges more clearly. These findings do not mean that there is a direct predisposition to be a believer or an atheist – but that there exist dispositions for a configuration of characteristics which, in interaction with the environment, facilitate religion or irreligion. As recent studies have shown, the genetic influences on religiosity partly overlap with the genetic influences on key, for religiosity, personality dispositions: agreeableness, low aggression, the need to belong, and the need to reduce uncertainty.

Finally, an intriguing question regarding personality characteristics of religiosity is the following: Do believers look to religion for ways to feel *humble*, i.e. admire others' qualities and accurately evaluate themselves, *self-effaced*, i.e. worse than others, or *self-enhanced*, i.e. worthy and better than others? In studies using the HEXACO personality model, which includes a sixth personality factor, i.e. honesty-humility, religious people, in their self-reports, tend to score high on honesty-humility.[11] However, as far as real humility is concerned, recent studies by Jochen Gebauer, Constantine Sedikides, and collaborators have suggested that Christians, and Westerners who practice yoga or meditation, tend to be narcissistic and self-enhanced in considering themselves better than others – in fact the average co-religionist – at least in domains that are central for their religious identity such as moral qualities that are normative within their religion.[12] Self-enhancing in domains central for the self is thus a universal principle in human functioning, including for the religious.

COGNITION, RELIGIOUS BELIEFS, AND RELIGIOSITY

Many religious beliefs are implausible, counterintuitive, or clearly irrational. They are unproved, unprovable, or clearly go against scientific evidence. Examples from Christianity are a Trinity God, religious miracles, and the virgin birth of Jesus. This constitutes a key difference of religion not only from science, but also from philosophy, where doubt is essential. Not surprisingly thus, religious believers have been suspected to be irrational and even low in intelligence.

The empirical research provides a more nuanced picture regarding the previously mentioned suspicion. There is indeed evidence, across cultures, that the proportion of nonbelievers among scientists is much higher than that among the general population. Also, across studies, religiosity is slightly higher among less educated individuals – but having attended religious versus public schools often constitutes an advantage for academic performance, possibly because of the conscientiousness-related values associated with religion. Similarly, at least in monotheistic cultures, religious believers tend to attribute low importance to science and rationality.[13] Furthermore, there is cross-cultural evidence indicating some negative associations between religiosity and intelligence. In addition, religious people have been found, in various places including the liberal Sweden, to show a propensity to accept pseudo-profound "bullshit" statements. These are seemingly impressive assertions that are presented with a syntactic structure, as true and meaningful, but are actually vacuous, with no discernible meaning (e.g. "Wholeness quiets infinite phenomena" or "Your movement transforms universal observations").[14]

However, other evidence prevents us from concluding in favor of an unambiguous link between religion and irrationality. First, a deeper examination of the negative link between religiosity and intelligence across cultures has shown that much of this effect is explained by lower educational levels and a lower quality of human conditions.[15] Second, rather than intelligence as a global cognitive dimension, a key difference between believers and nonbelievers is their style of thinking. Across cultural contexts, religious people tend to prefer intuitive and holistic thinking and global, non-detailed, perception, while nonbelievers embrace an analytic thinking style.[16] Whereas analytic thinking is central and critical in rationality and science, holistic thinking is not totally irrational, unscientific, or unproductive, and may actually have a heuristic value in terms of discovering new things and enhancing creativity.[17]

Third, though isolated studies may show either positive or negative links between religiosity and (nonreligious) paranormal beliefs, more integrative research shows a nuanced and interesting "big picture." Both atheists and those who are highly religious dislike paranormal beliefs – probably for different reasons. It is, in contrast, those who are moderately religious who also endorse paranormal beliefs.[18] This may perhaps help to understand why the major world religions have been successful in number and duration compared to weird groups that are limited in size, such as apocalyptic or satanic cults. As Pascal Boyer has suggested, the major world religions have retained only a few minimally counterintuitive elements in their beliefs compared to the degree and extent of irrationality in the beliefs of weird cults.[19] Moreover, these counterintuitive elements have usually received, within the religious communities, a moral interpretation and do not stand alone as eccentric manifestations of God's supra-natural abilities. For instance, a Trinity God denotes the importance for humans to be united even if different; and biblical miracles mostly involve a healing of human suffering.

WOMEN AND MEN

Women are typically more religious than men and this holds across most cultures and religions. This difference is clearer when one focuses on the individual aspect of religiosity (belief, prayer) compared to the social aspect, i.e. affiliation and collective practice – there may be social norms in some religions favoring men's participation in public religious practice. How can we understand women's stronger religious belief and attitudes?

Sociological reasons that have been proposed to explain this difference include traditional gender roles and related differences between men and women in work and attachment to family values and children's education. These factors play some limited role: the gender differences in religiosity diminish in more modern societies disposing of higher gender equality and social security. However, these factors are not sufficient explanations since in modern and secular societies, women are still more religious.

Thus, psychological differences, in terms of personality and cognition, contribute to, if not explain, women's stronger interest in religion.[20] Indeed, women tend to be more agreeable and conscientious, or lower in psychoticism, than men. Similar tendencies are found for values, with women placing greater priority than men on self-transcendent values (benevolence and universalism) and men more strongly endorsing values opposing conservation. These differences extend to more focused ones, with men being, for instance, more aggressive and impulsive and greater risk-takers. In addition, women, compared to men, tend to use more intuitive and holistic thinking and less analytic thinking. Though small in size, these gender differences seem pervasive, beyond the role of culture, development, and generation. Thus, religious faith and values are more attractive to people who are concerned with quality in interpersonal relations and personal and societal stability, and those who have a more globalized perception of reality. Consequently, religion is more appealing to women than men, and more appealing to men with these specific personality and cognitive tendencies.

SPECIFIC FORMS: SPIRITUALITY, FUNDAMENTALISM, AND EMOTIONALITY-BASED RELIGION

If the coexistence of agreeableness and conscientiousness characterizes religiosity in general, the combination of agreeableness, and possibly conscientiousness, with another personality disposition predicts some specific forms of expressing religious and spiritual inclinations such as modern spirituality, fundamentalism, and emotion-based religion.

SPIRITUALITY

The combination of agreeableness and the personality dimension of *openness to experience* characterizes, and predicts in the long term, what we call today modern spirituality. Modern spirituality denotes the individual search for meaning and interconnectedness with others and the world through the belief in a transcendent entity or princi-ple, not necessarily within the framework of, or even independently from, established religious traditions and institutions.[21]

People who place high value on quality in interpersonal relation-ships and who are open to alternative, complex, and creative ways of thinking and experiencing the life's everyday reality are attracted to modern spirituality. This combination of agreeableness and openness to experience also implies universalistic values. The prosocial orien-tation is not limited to proximal people but is more extensive and embraces the world. Similarly, being religious or spiritual in a secular country, where secularism and irreligion are normative, may reflect a personality disposition to "swim against the stream" and be different, by being interested in an alternative consideration of the everyday life that is, for instance, less materialistic and less focused on self-interest. Moreover, modern spirituality shares with traditional religiosity the preference for holistic over analytic thinking, but the nonreligious forms of modern individualized spirituality tend to attract people with inclinations toward some aspects of paranormal thinking and experience (e.g. magical ideation, dissociation).[22]

FUNDAMENTALISM

Environmental as well as genetic influences play a role not only in gen-eral religiosity, but also in the way one is religious. This also applies to fundamentalism. Religious people may turn out to be fundamental-ists, first, because of socialization and their family's intergenerational transmission of authoritarian, conservative, and dogmatic forms of religion. Second, the personality dispositions favoring fundamentalist religiosity are agreeableness and conscientiousness (as for religiosity) combined with *low openness to experience*. Finally, specific contextual factors activate and boost more radicalized forms of religion.

At the socio-cognitive level, fundamentalists seem to be religious people who accentuate the tendencies of common religiosity to an excessive degree. The religious need for order, structure, and answers in the inner and external world thus becomes *dogmatism*, i.e. the denial of evidence disconfirming one's own ideas; *literalism*, i.e. the intra-textual, nonsymbolic, and selective understanding of religious content; *orthodoxy*, i.e. the obeying of sources of religious authority without questioning; *dualism* in black-and-white thinking; *moralization*, with all issues and decisions becoming subject of moral judgment; and *rigorism*, with religious conviction prevailing over moral conviction.[23]

NEUROTIC VERSUS "HEALTHY-MINDED" RELIGION

As seen in the previous chapter, in the beginning of the 20th century, William James described two types of religiosity. One, called by James "sick soul," is based on the perception of turmoil in human existence and of the presence of something inherently evil in life and the world. The other, called "healthy-minded," is animated by the joy of existence and broad optimism.[24]

In continuation to some extent with this distinction, we can conceive first that, if the other conditions mentioned previously in this chapter are met (environmental availability of religion, agreeable and conscientious inclinations), then, those who are additionally *highly neurotic/emotionally unstable*, i.e. anxious, depressed, or guilt stricken, may be inclined to live religious experiences marked by emotional negativity and negative religious ideas such as belief in a punishing God or a threatening devil. Alternatively, these individuals may look for highly emotionally supportive religious groups, especially ones of small size, such as several new religious movements, which provide affection and emotional stability. Also, as shown by some longitudinal studies, socialized religious people who are also neurotic may end up exiting from religion and abandoning faith. Neurotic people are suspected to be more sensitive when facing particularly negative life situations. These situations may accentuate a negative God concept and perceptions of injustice in the world or of moral hypocrisy of significant others. Second, again when the other conditions are met (religion in the environment, agreeableness and conscientiousness), those individuals who are additionally *high in positive emotionality*, i.e. low in neuroticism and high in extraversion, may be attracted by charismatic and extraverted forms of religious expression.[25]

Interestingly, the previously mentioned differences between religious expressions based on negative versus positive emotionality can be found not only between individuals, but also between cultures. For instance, several studies suggest slight differences between US Christianity, in particular US contemporary Protestantism, and European Christianity, in particular Catholicism. The latter is historically marked by an emphasis on sin and guilt, whereas, in the US, religious people tend to be marked by positive emotionality in their personality.[26]

SIGNIFICANT LIFE EXPERIENCES

Religious socialization and personality characteristics may have a rather stable influence on current religiosity and its forms. However, people may also experience slight or important changes in their religious trajectory. These changes occur following more certain situations and significant life events. Classically, such situations and events that have been studied by psychologists and sociologists are those that imply deprivation and vulnerability in various life domains and affecting various aspects of the self. Nevertheless, more recently, psychologists have also started to identify the role that positive personal experiences play on religious and spiritual changes.

NEGATIVE LIFE EVENTS AND THREATS TO THE SELF

A prototypical situation of vulnerability is the activation of the perspective of mortality. Experimental studies in the framework of the

Terror Management Theory have shown that, when participants are asked to think of their death and write a few sentences, they tend afterwards to report a stronger belief in God – and even in gods of religions other than their own. Nonbelievers have been found to do the same – at least at an implicit, not very conscious, level. In addition, as other experiments have shown, strong religious believers are somehow immune to the other typical effects of this manipulation that make mortality salient: they experience less of an increased need for self-esteem or for defense of cultural values.[27]

Beyond death, several negative life events and situations at the individual or societal level may constitute threats to specific aspects of the self, such as self-esteem, self-control, certainty, meaning, and order. Typical examples are the loss of a loved one, divorce, a professional or financial crisis, a serious illness – especially when the causes and outcomes are unclear, traumatic experiences, persecution, and discrimination. These negative events and situations, which considerably affect the self, can motivate individuals to change their religious trajectories by converting, de-converting, switching, or discovering a vocation in life.

Moreover, as research by Pehr Granqvist, Lee Kirkpatrick, and other researchers has shown, longer lasting negative situations at the relational level, mainly the experience of insecure (low quality) attachment to parents in childhood or to the loved partner in adulthood, are facilitators, if not elicitors, of significant, sometimes dramatic, changes in one's own religious and spiritual trajectory. In these cases, people need religion, a loving God, and/or a supportive community to find or restore attachment security. Alternatively, people may exit from faith due to their insecure attachment or as an indirect form of protest. Similarly, parents' divorce often negatively affects individual religiousness and facilitates religious disaffiliation/de-conversion or change of denomination.[28]

Interestingly, the previously mentioned accumulated evidence comes not only from studies on the impact of life events and societal phenomena, but also from dozens of recent experimental studies in the lab. In those studies, the experimenter induces threat to some aspect of the self (esteem, control, certainty, meaning, order, attachment security), for instance by having the participant read a relevant short text or receive fictitious feedback. It appears that when participants experience, even for few minutes, such hypothetical vulnerability in one of the previously mentioned areas, they tend to more strongly endorse religious beliefs, in particular the belief in a powerful and/or loving God, are more inclined to perform religious rituals, or self-identify more strongly with their religion. Additionally, as in the studies on the effects of mortality salience, very religious participants are often found to feel less threatened by the manipulations in such experiments. Interestingly, if alternates to religious solutions (e.g. the activation of the idea of a strong state government, or interpretation of the absurd artistic work) are provided in these experiments to restore meaning, self-control, or self-esteem, participants are less inclined to use religion as a refuge.

However, religion provides several specific characteristics that render its attractiveness particularly appealing and possibly unique in situations of significant distress. Religious beliefs, compared to other kinds of beliefs and ideas, are powerful because they are simultaneously characterized by unfalsifiability; limited eccentricity (i.e. few counterintuitive elements); anthropomorphism in believing in a just, loving, and protecting supreme being; and promises for literal immortality.[29]

POSITIVE EMOTIONAL EXPERIENCES AND SELF-TRANSCENDENCE

Anecdotal evidence as well as psychological studies favor the idea that people convert to faith or receive a "vocational call" most frequently following a significant *negative* experience *affecting the self*, such as an insecure attachment history or the loss of a loved one, and, less so after disasters affecting others. Moreover, there are not many conversions or vocational narratives following strong *positive* experiences, especially those related to *the self and its expansion*, such as being accepted into a prestigious university, winning the lottery, having extraordinary summer vacations, or having sex with the most beautiful/handsome, funny, and intelligent partner.

Nevertheless, there is some anecdotal evidence indicating that people may convert or intensify their religious and spiritual inclinations after specific *positive emotional experiences* that allow for some sort of *self-transcendence*. For instance, according to the legend, Russians converted to Christianity after their representatives were marveled by the byzantine ritual in the famous basilica of Saint Sophia in Constantinople. Furthermore, several Westerners of monotheistic religious tradition convert to Buddhism as they find it to be a spirituality that clearly promotes the abolishment of ingroup versus outgroup barriers and unambiguously sustains universalistic values.

Interestingly, in recent years, several experimental studies in our and other laboratories and other scholarly works have indicated that when people experience specific kinds of positive emotions that are stimulus- or other-oriented, such as awe, artistic beauty, moral elevation, or compassion, but not self-oriented (e.g. personal joy, pride), their spiritual and religious aspirations, attitudes, and even behaviors are activated or become more prominent. This can be interpreted in several ways. Experiencing these kinds of emotions broadens the self, which is confronted with a vaster and more important reality. The self may even be experienced as diminished and integrated into a more global reality due to increased feelings of oneness with others; time constraints that appear less pressing; experiential and nonmaterialistic values that gain prominence; and a life and world that appear to be, respectively, more meaningful and more benevolent.[30]

CONCLUSION

People may be religious believers or atheists primarily due to their earlier (ir)religious family socialization, in particular by that of their mothers, but also grandparents, in particular grandmothers, and other family members. The impact of this religious socialization is enhanced by a caring and nonauthoritarian style of parenting, parental homogamy (i.e. similarity with respect to religious issues), strong societal secularism, and the religious group's possible minority status. External sources of socialization, such as peers, mentors, and institutions, may solidify or fragilize the familial religious socialization.

Beyond the role of socialization, people with personality tendencies emphasizing quality in interpersonal relationships, and order and stability in the internal and external world, and having – perhaps consequently – a strong need for epistemic closure and a preference for intuitive and holistic over analytic thinking, are more attracted by religious faiths, practices, norms, and communities (but not by paranormal beliefs), which promote and celebrate the corresponding ideals. The previously mentioned trends seem to also explain genetic influences on (ir)religiosity, which are more powerful in young adulthood than in earlier ages, as well as the fact that women exhibit stronger faith and religious practice compared to men. Those who are additionally very open to experience look for modern spiritual forms as an alternative to traditional religion; and those who, on the contrary, are reluctant to new, unconventional, and complex ideas, values, and experiences, feel more comfortable within fundamentalist groups. Neurotic personality tendencies, i.e. emotional instability and negativity, among those who are religiously socialized facilitate religious turmoil or exit from religion.

Finally, emotional and relational vulnerability, whether stable, such as a history of insecure attachment with parents or partners, or more limited in time, such as negative life events and mortality salience, or finally simply induced by experimenters in the lab, push people to take refuge in religion as a means to restore emotional stability, relational security, perceived immortality, and meaning and control in life. Nevertheless, some kinds of positive emotional experiences that allow for a decentralization of the self or an admiration of an inspiring stimulus, and thus create a sense of self-transcendence, also have the capacity to enhance religious and spiritual aspirations.

3

THEIST CHILDREN, APOSTATE ADOLESCENTS, BIGOT LATE ADULTS?

It is often assumed that children are credulous, show propensity for magical thinking, and should thus be naturally oriented to believe in God, angels, afterlife, and miracles. Adolescents and young adults, as rebels and doubters, should be prone to distance themselves, and even exit, from religion. Late adults, seeing the perspective of death approaching, are believed to look to religion as a way to guarantee immortality. In line with the stereotype of human development as a life cycle where humans return to a childlike state in old age, the elderly should end up as bigots – churches indeed are full of old women and men.

Are the previously mentioned assumptions true? As we will see in this chapter, these assumptions are not completely false, but they tell only half of the story. The opposite of the trends mentioned earlier may also be true, with children being open to atheism, adolescents to spirituality, adults to magical thinking, and elderly adults to secularism. Moreover, human development concerns not only religious believing, but also bonding, behaving, and belonging. Cognitive, emotional, moral, and social developmental changes, even if interdependent, follow partly distinct trajectories. The chapter will focus extensively on childhood, given the intriguing questions it poses for our understanding of how religion emerges in individuals' lives, but it will also examine how religiosity develops in adolescence, adulthood, and late adulthood.

ARE CHILDREN NATURALLY OR CULTURALLY (A)THEISTS?

The question of whether children are naturally oriented to religion or not is more complex than it appears at first glance. Being naturally predisposed to religion or, more broadly, spirituality, by being equipped with some inherent categories like the belief in a transcendent entity, is different from being receptive to religious ideas if the latter are culturally presented as real. Moreover, such receptiveness is slightly different from the question of whether children are *more* receptive to religion than nonbelief, if both are culturally normative. Finally, children's psychological function does not mean stronger natural influences compared to adults. As we saw in Chapter 2, genetic influences on personality and religiosity are more evident in young adulthood. Additionally, adults may think as children, and children may be less childish than we imagine.

BELIEFS AND COGNITIVE DEVELOPMENT

CHILDREN'S FAITH AS NOT SO CHILDISH

People intuitively think that children are naturally inclined to be credulous, endorse magical thinking, and easily hold counterintuitive and paranormal beliefs, i.e. ones that go against humans', including children's, naïve psychology and physics built into their experience with the physical and social world. Two underlying assumptions are that this is the case because of children's cognitive limitations and their natural inclination toward fantasy and the extraordinary.

Indeed, from an old perspective of cognitive development where aging implies access to new and more advanced modes of thought and the abandon of older ones, it has been found in older research, from the 1960s to the 1990s, that children's and adolescents' beliefs and faith develop accordingly as they age. They progressively become more abstract, symbolic, internalized, individualized, and relativistic, and less concrete, literal, simply adopted, and absolutistic.[1]

However, while not entirely refuting the previously mentioned, more recent research over the last 20 years has provided important nuances to these assumptions. Children are less irrational and adults less rational than previously thought. Children are more capable of distinguishing between fantasy and reality than we intuitively tend to think: when hungry, they do not request a cookie from their imaginary friend. Moreover, magical thinking in childhood is not only a cognitive limitation, but also a powerful heuristic tool for exploration and creativity. Furthermore, adults do not really abandon older modes of thinking: old and new modes coexist and, in situations such as personal crises, the older ways of thinking come back. Similarly, adults continue to have an anthropomorphic perception of God, even if to a lesser degree than children. Though they endorse the theologically correct idea that God is omnipresent, adults think and feel as if God is too occupied with others' prayers and thus too distant to listen their own requests.[2]

In addition, religious beliefs are not totally unique cognitions, coming out from nowhere, and being totally irrational. They are built on, extend, and presuppose, even when transgressing, children's everyday social cognition. Belief in God's omniscience presupposes the acquisition of the theory of mind, i.e. the ability to attribute mental states – knowledge, intents, and emotions – to oneself and to others, and to understand that others have beliefs, desires, intentions, and perspectives that are different from one's own. Belief in the afterlife requires that a child understands the biology of death, i.e. how the end of the life cycle implies the end of vital processes, and belief in a guardian angel parallels a child's relationship with an imaginary companion.[3]

Finally, religious beliefs, contrary to nonreligious paranormal beliefs, include few counterintuitive elements and many realistic ones.

Research by Ara Norenzayan and colleagues shows that legends with few counterintuitive elements in an otherwise plausible story have a better chance to be remembered and transmitted, compared to stories that are either too ordinary or too bizarre.[4] Moreover, whereas religious and nonreligious, scientific, explanations of reality (e.g. of how the world was made) may be antagonistic in one's mind, they may also simply coexist, and do so among both children and adults.[5]

CHILDREN'S SKEPTICISM AND ADULTS' RELIGIOUS TESTIMONY

Are children naturally inclined to believe in God, an afterlife, and miracles, or are religious beliefs essentially endorsed by children because of social transmission? Recent research confirms the second. Contrary to what has been sometimes argued, children do not come into the world with a disposition for a special conceptual category for "God": for very young children, God, like humans, is also fallible, has limited knowledge, and may hold debatable moral beliefs.[6] That research sheds light on the intriguing question of how children deal with claims made by adults regarding facts that are not observable and are even counterintuitive, going against children's intuitive knowledge of the physical and psychological world. Note that such adults' "testimony" includes not only religious beliefs but also scientific knowledge (e.g. evolutionism) that may go against what we naively think (e.g. all of our ancestors should have been humans).

In fact, as research by Paul Harris, collaborators, and other researchers has shown, an interaction takes place between (1) the child's individual characteristics, including age, psychological characteristics, religious culture, and prior knowledge based on her experience of the physical and the psychological world; (2) the adult messengers' characteristics, including their status and the quality of their relationship with the child; and (3) the very nature of the religious claim made and the way it is expressed. At first glance, children are puzzled when adults present them as being real elements that challenge their assumption that there are natural causal regularities constraining what can possibly happen in the world. As children grow, for instance, four years old compared to three years old, they become even more skeptical. We will examine next the role of religious culture, quality of child-adult relationship, and the way counterintuitive ideas are presented.

First, children who have not received a religious education doubt that violations of ordinary causal constraints can ever happen, whereas Christian and Muslim children who have received a religious education are more likely to believe that miracles can occur. Similarly, children in more religious cultures are less skeptical compared to other cultures. Thus, amazingly, whereas older children can be more skeptical, those who are religiously socialized develop, as they grow, better representations of the unseen and counterintuitive ideas and events. They develop an ability to visualize or imagine them, which in turn makes these phenomena more believable.

Second, children will be more trusting of testimony about religious and other counterintuitive ideas if the adults (parents, teachers, experts) presenting this testimony have authority and knowledge and are persons with whom the children entertain a positive relationship. Trust and social motives are possibly more important than epistemic motives: children may endorse religious ideas, not necessarily because they believe them, but because the adult who presents them as real is someone with whom children would like to affiliate.

Third, strange ideas, beings, and events that are presented as plausible, are announced as "going to be surprising" (rather than just letting the child wonder what is going on), are introduced in a realistic everyday context rather than a fantastic context, and are confirmed by several others, have a better chance to be well received by children. Finally, it is important to consider that, beyond all of these factors, children, even the very skeptical and knowledgeable, tend to be somewhat fascinated by the unexpected and counterintuitive.[7]

Thus, one should not conclude that religious socialization by adults violates children's natural tendency for skepticism; or that children simply trust whatever adults tell them. Religious ideas find in children, like in adults, plenty of room to flourish. For instance, children "over-detect" intentionality: things, and the world too, exist as the result of someone's intentions and are not just artifacts. Pre-schoolers believe that positive or neutral events are more likely than negative events to occur in real life; they thus have no strong reason to dismiss Santa Claus's visit. Finally, assuming a body versus soul/mind dualism, and believing that grandparents will be in heaven forever, is more comforting than accepting that they are just dead and gone.[8]

RITUALS AND EMOTIONAL, RELATIONAL, AND SOCIAL DEVELOPMENT

Research on the cognitive aspects of children's religion has been extensive, probably because of the emphasis of Western Protestant-ism on belief and faith. On the contrary, the role religious rituals, emotions, and the community may have on children's development is understudied, with a notable exception being research on religion and attachment.

AWE AND GOD AS LOVING AND JUDGING

The religious child's emotional world and relationship to God closely resemble Freud's description of religion as reflecting the child's emotional bond with the "imaginary father," fantasized as being both loving/protecting and judging/punishing. Research on God rep-resentations has partly confirmed Freud's idea: God's image combines the loving and judging aspects in adults' and children's minds, and there is a noteworthy correspondence between parental images and God images. Nevertheless, the image of loving, rather than punishing, God has today become increasingly preponderant.[9]

The previously mentioned Freudian conception of God and reli-gion also evokes the emotion of awe, i.e. a fascination and rever-ence when confronted with a stimulus of vastness or a being of power and importance. Religious and spiritual experiences produce, as described by Rudolph Otto in the 19th century, the feeling of a *mysterium tremendum et fascinans.* As also mentioned in Chapter 2, experiencing awe can elicit spiritual aspirations. Though research on this topic is still to come, it is reasonable to assume that awe is a central emotion in the child's experience of the sacred, particularly through religious rituals, objects, and figures, as well as extraordinary legends and miracles.

TRUST AND SECURE ATTACHMENT TO GOD AND THE WORLD

Similarly to some extent, but by focusing exclusively on the positive side of the relationship, it has been argued and found, from an attachment theory perspective, that God functions like the child's attachment figure. This figure is the caregiver who provides love, is sought for protection in moments of adversity, and is trusted as a secure base that allows for exploration. The use of God as an additional or substitute attachment figure requires that the child has developed the cognitive capacity to attach to more abstract and invisible figures.

Research from this perspective has mostly confirmed a *correspondence* model underlying the success of religious socialization. Children in religious families who have developed a secure parental attachment generalize this positive relational model by extending it to God and religious figures and the community with whom a similarly secure and trusting relationship is developed. Inversely, insecure – anxious, ambivalent, or avoidant – attachment that develops when parents' warmth and support are inconsistent, changing, or undetectable may generalize to a negative relationship with an insecure God. Moreover, in a *compensation* model, children in religious families who have developed an insecure attachment to parents may find a shelter of security and love in God and religion. The religious discourse presents God as a figure who loves unconditionally, values every person, and protects. As experiments by Pehr Granqvist and other researchers have shown, religious children increase their proximity to God when their attachment security is threatened.[10]

The coexistence of these two models does not imply that the theory predicts anything: children in religious families who have developed a secure attachment to their parents have no reason to develop negative God perceptions and negative religious attitudes. Trust is thus a central dimension, in addition to awe, that underlies the religious child's relationship to religion. Moreover, religious rituals imply that being in contact with God enhances one's connectedness with others and the world. A child's religion contributes to a more global trust of others and the world. Perhaps not surprisingly, as data from 16 European countries show, religious adults show stronger social trust than nonbelievers, i.e. they believe that others are trustworthy, fair, and helpful.[11]

RELATEDNESS AND PRAYER

The major world religions dispose of gods whose main characteristic is that they have an intellect and a psychology similar to humans. They may not have a body, but they know things that are important for us and our lives, have feelings and desires, behave accordingly, and interact with us. In addition, God is perceived as having human qualities at a higher level, be they cognitive (omniscience), emotional (secondary, exclusively human, emotions, but not primary, animal-like, human emotions), or related to personality (highest scores in positive personality traits).[12] Communicating frequently through individual and collective prayer with such a supreme being, even if invisible, may be appealing and useful, more so than communicating with other invisible beings, ghosts, and even our dead loved ones.

Some research findings on the developmental aspects of children's prayer are worth mentioning. Older research, inspired by Jean Piaget's theory on the stages of cognitive development, has suggested that children's prayer evolves from a mechanical repetition of formulas to concrete requests and then to the expression of more abstract goals.[13] Recent research has shown that even preschoolers of three to four years old already believe that God is, compared to humans, more aware of people's expressed needs, even if these needs are expressed silently. Nevertheless, the distinction between God's and humans' awareness increases as children become older. Other research has shown that four- and six-year-old children perceive prayer as being motivated only by positive emotions, whereas older children realize that negative emotions also cause people to pray and that prayer helps them feel better. Moreover, though petitionary prayer, i.e. making requests to God, is present in both early childhood and later ages, other kinds of prayer such as conversation with God or expression of gratitude become more present in prayer as children become older.[14]

Finally, as Jacqueline Woolley has argued and found, there may exist a developmental trend from magical thinking, to wishing, and then to prayer. The early magical thinking ("I can, with my thought, modify the external reality") is replaced, by three to four years, by the activity of wishing. The latter, though still marked by the belief in mental-physical causality, is qualitatively different: children are able to distinguish between reality and fantasy and are progressively aware that wishing may not be efficient. Then, in older children raised in religious families, prayer represents a continuation of the function of wishing, but does so in qualitatively different and more complex terms. The expected effect of the mental activity on desired changes passes through a personal relationship with God with whom one has to negotiate. Given the realism with which the supernatural is socially presented, older religious children increasingly believe in the efficiency of prayer.[15]

RELIGIOUS IDENTIFICATION AND INTERGROUP RELATIONS

Religious ideas and affects are already present in the life of preschoolers receiving religious socialization (four- to five-year-olds) and continue to develop over the following years. During ages 6 to 11, very likely due to school experiences and participation in public religious activities, children, be they of majority or minority religion, progressively acquire identification with their own religious group – slightly later than their identification with their ethnic/national group. Then, children begin to endorse the parents' and the group's (negative) stereotypes about other religious groups, including atheists, and develop certain ingroup preferences and possibly outgroup derogation. This is more explicitly observable in schoolchildren, compared to adolescents and adults who may be better able to hide negative attitudes toward religious outgroups or, alternatively, mature and develop intergroup tolerance and understanding.[16]

RELIGION DETRIMENTAL FOR CHILDREN: CULTS, FUNDAMENTALISM, AND ABUSIVE CLERGY

The religiosity of parents, family, and children may have positive effects on children's mental health and well-being, especially in situations of adversity. Alternatively, religiosity may simply be unrelated to the well-being of children, such effects becoming more distinguishable in adolescence and adulthood. However, some specific religious contexts constitute risks for children's well-being and optimal development, if not for mental health. This is the case of belonging to detrimental new religious movements, being raised in fundamentalist families, and encounters with clergy members with sexual perversions.

NEW RELIGIOUS MOVEMENTS AND FUNDAMENTALIST FAMILIES

New religious movements, called cults when clearly detrimental, are typically groups of small size that exist at the margins of society and have some unconventional or questionable beliefs and practices. There is no clear or strong evidence that being raised with parents who are fundamentalists or who belong to a new religious movement is necessarily detrimental for children's mental health and well-being. Moreover, when they become adults, several of these children may develop the capacity to distance themselves from and exit such groups.[17]

Nevertheless, what seems clear is that parental education, or the broader socialization in these families and communities, is highly restrictive; places value on obedience; uses punitiveness occasionally including physical abuse, even if possibly coupled with expressions of warmth and love; and creates subcultures opposing the broader society. All of this reflects authoritarian tendencies, legitimated by fundamentalist, conspirational, and antisocial religious ideas. They can affect children's optimal and maturational development by favoring low cognitive flexibility, high dualistic thinking, fear-, guilt-, and disgust-motivated morality, and low autonomy and creativity.[18] Of particular concern are the long-term negative consequences, such as depression, suicidal thoughts, and suicide attempts, that homophobic education in these environments has on children and adolescents who develop a minority sexual orientation.[19]

CLERGY'S SEXUAL ABUSE

Minors', most often adolescents', sexual abuse by clergy has not been a negligible phenomenon. Even if such cases are proportionally few with respect to the total number of clergy, or not more frequent than in the general population, they are numerous and serious for professionals with sacred and high moral ideals and low criminal scores in other issues. Though religious beliefs, rituals, norms, and community do not have, strictly speaking, a direct causal role here, the religious context presents features that facilitate such behavior by persons with sexually abusive dispositions.

The first of these facilitating features is structural and exists in a variety of settings that consist of a concentration of minors who have asymmetrical relationships with adult educators. Second, within a religious environment, the facilitating factors specifically include: clergy's immature and repressed sexuality, which is religiously legitimized through ideals of chastity and the belief in women's inferiority; same-sex male attraction and the problematic dating and sexual experiences that clergy members encountered prior to or during the seminary; experiencing religion primarily as power, possibly doubled with a rhetoric of God's love; and a "moral licensing" effect, where doing or preaching the good diminishes priests' moral immunity and resistance to temptations.

Additional factors favor low reporting and institutional silencing. Religious individuals – family, victims, and other potential witnesses – tend, because of their personality and values, to be trusting of others in general and of co-religionists and clergy in particular. They may justify and tolerate clergy's abuse, sometimes through self-blaming or by blaming the victim. Finally, religious authorities have adopted defensive attitudes that have prioritized the institution's interests and minimized and ignored the facts and allegations.[20]

ARE ADOLESCENTS APOSTATES AND LATE ADULTS BIGOTS?

Childhood offers the first basis for the development of positive, negative, or neutral and indifferent attitudes toward religion and spirituality. Religious and spiritual attitudes and trajectories in the subsequent stages of life are not new chapters to be written on a white page but constitute developments and re-elaborations of the child's first approach to faith, practice, and religious belonging. To fully understand the life span development of religiosity, one has to distinguish, as is also the case for other aspects of human development, between three independent and complementary dynamics: *developmental changes*, *cohort effects*, and *interindividual variability* implying stability and/or change.

First, as people age, changes at the mean level of personal characteristics are observed. In parallel, adolescents, on average, may become more skeptical, whereas elderly adults, again in general, more practicing religion. Second, societal changes and events affect people and groups. Those born in the late 1990s and 2000s (generation Z) constitute a different cohort from those born in the 1960s and 1970s (generation X). In the West, the latter grew up in societies that were about to secularize rapidly; the former grew up in a post-9/11 world, where secularists were trying to understand why religious identities are so pervasive and powerful. Finally, individuals, even those in the same cohort or age group, differ from each other. Some are very religious and others less or not at all. Will these differences persist across the life span? Indeed, the life span stability in individuals' religious variability is more important in size than the change. As they age, several people convert, and many become atheists, but most people remain similarly religious or irreligious, and do so for many decades. The central focus of the next sections will be on the first dynamic, i.e. developmental changes.

ADOLESCENCE AND EMERGING ADULTHOOD: A CRITICAL AGE FOR ATHEISM OR SPIRITUALITY?

Early adolescence brings considerable biological changes, accompanied by changes in the cognitive, emotional, relational, moral, and social levels of later adolescence and emerging adulthood. Body and body image change, and sexuality takes an important place. The ability for abstract thinking is solidified; the need for autonomy presses for distance from the family's world and for openness to other sources of socialization; and concerns for self-esteem increase, notably with respect to issues such as attractiveness, intimacy, and group acceptance. The capacity for more coherent and autonomous moral thinking grows, and questions about identity, meaning, and one's purpose in life emerge, be they in concrete terms (e.g. future professional orientation) or more global existential terms (Who am I? What must my generation do in this world?). There are also slight changes in basic personality dimensions. For biological, social, and possibly evolutionary reasons, adolescents become slightly less agreeable and conscientious, and more open to experience. Clearly, this is a time for exploring alternatives.

DECLINE OR TRANSFORMATION OF RELIGIOSITY

Not surprisingly thus, adolescence and emerging adulthood are age periods of questioning and possible changes in attitudes toward religion and spirituality. As noted earlier, a major trend is the continuation of being religious or not. However, there is a specific effect of age that is not reducible to education, on a certain, though not dramatic, decline in religious attendance and, to a lesser degree, in religious belief and affiliation. Spirituality declines much less. This decline is due to age and is not an artifact of a cohort effect: it is consistent across cohorts and has been confirmed longitudinally. Moreover, the decline is more plausible, or occurs earlier, among those with moderately religious parents compared to those coming from very religious families.[21]

The aforementioned specific developmental changes at this age are responsible for doubting, distancing oneself, and in turn exiting from religion. Religious beliefs appear implausible, rituals make little room for individuality and creativity, a family's ideology will be questioned, and external influences will increase. Moral inconsistencies of religious professionals become troubling, sexuality and experiential openness need to be expressed rather than restricted, and the self-concept has to be reworked with autonomy.[22]

Nevertheless, some other, although fewer, adolescents will react by reaffirming or qualitatively reworking their religiosity. This includes the possibility of faith maturation, experiencing a vocational religious and moral call, shifting from literal, orthodox, and institutional forms of religion to symbolic, questing, and spiritual ones; or the opposite, i.e. radicalization. For all of the previously mentioned, mentors and moral and spiritual exemplary figures often play a significant role. For some older adolescents, turning to religion may be a reaction to a secular world perceived as unjust, materialistic, and too rational. Moreover, turning to nonreligious spirituality probably prevents young adults from throwing the baby (i.e. the belief in a transcendent entity, the feeling of interconnection with all beings, and the conviction that life and the world are meaningful) out with the bath water, i.e. the institutional aspects of religion.[23]

It may be interesting to give one indicative example from a recent analysis of US data on 12,000 individuals from the National Longitudinal Study of Adolescent to Adult Health. Whereas 50 percent of the studied sample ended up remaining, from adolescence to adulthood through young adulthood, stable (in being religious, 19 percent; non-religious, 15 percent; or religiously affiliated but religiously inactive, 16 percent), 40 percent of them experienced a decline in their religiosity, either definitively (24 percent) or temporarily (16 percent returned to religion in their 30s; see a later section). Only 10 percent became increasingly more religious after adolescence.[24]

RELIGION, IDENTITY, AND SEXUALITY

Two developmental tasks have been theorized as being central for adolescence and emerging adulthood: identity formation and sexual maturation. Religion affects and is affected by both.

First, as postulated in Erikson's theory of psychosocial development, this age implies defining one's own personal identity – in general, with regard to the individual within the world, and across specific life domains. Many adolescents dedicate effort and time to exploration: this identity status is called *moratorium*. Others, after exploration, commit to a new or reworked identity: this identity status is called *achievement*. Finally, others will just adopt a *foreclosed* identity, i.e. commitment but without exploration.

In a review of 20 studies across various countries, it appeared that adolescents' and young adults' religiosity is characterized primarily by commitment to identity formation. Whether this committed identity presupposes exploration or not, thus being achieved or foreclosed, depends on whether religiosity is questing and symbolic or, inversely, literal and traditional. High moratorium status is typical of doubters and the disaffiliated. Moreover, longitudinal studies in North America and Europe suggest that the relationship between religion and identity formation is reciprocal: changes in identity status influence later religious attitudes, but changes in religiosity also influence subsequent identity status.[25]

Second, from an evolutionary perspective of the pyramid of human needs and the respective developmental tasks, adolescence and emerging adulthood are considered to be marked by the need to find sexual mates and, next, the need to retain one. (The latter need parallels Erikson's developmental task of *intimacy* in young adulthood.) Research confirms though that religiosity and sexuality are somehow at odds. Religious adolescents and young adults, consistently across cultures, tend to have more restrictive and less permissive sexuality. These include negative attitudes and low practice relative to premarital sex, multiple partners, same-sex relationships, diversity of heterosexual behaviors, and having sex only for pleasure.[26] Longitudinal evidence confirms that the religion-sexuality conflict of youth persists long term. A decrease of religiosity was found to be followed by a later increase of sexual behavior. Inversely, the first sexual intercourse or pornography use were found to predict a later decrease of religious interests.[27]

ADULTHOOD AND LATE ADULTHOOD: A DIVERSITY OF PATHWAYS

Human development during the several decades of adulthood has been investigated in psychology to a lesser degree, compared to the previous ages. The same is true for the role of religion with regard to the developmental aspects of adults' lives. Nevertheless, some key trends are worthy of mention.

STATUS CHANGE: FROM RECIPIENT TO PROVIDER OF SERVICES

Most young adults and adults will get married, at least once, will have children, and will develop a professional career. In Erikson's terms, their major developmental task will be *generativity*, i.e. making their mark on their environment through producing, creating, and developing things and contributing to the growth of other people, in particular the young. For biological and social reasons, the mean levels of personality traits will experience meaningful changes – in the opposite direction compared to adolescence. Among others, agreeableness and conscientiousness will increase, whereas openness to experience will decrease.

Not surprisingly, the perspective and experience of family formation and parenthood may reactivate, to some extent, religious beliefs, practice, values, and/or belonging, and do so also among some of those who had distanced themselves from religion in the previous years. Educating children implies the responsibility of investing one's own resources, transmitting beliefs and values, and inserting them into a cultural community.[28] These goals may explain the religious "homogamy" we mentioned in Chapter 2: religion or irreligion is among the top similarities between future parents. During this period, we observe the phenomenon among parents with relatively low personal religious interests of providing their children with opportunities for some religious education or familiarization with religious culture. To give one example: secular nonbeliever American Jews will pass on the old religious rituals of circumcision and bar mitzvah to their sons.[29] Nevertheless, the solidification of personality differences between people, due to the stronger genetic influences at that age described in Chapter 2, will contribute to the stabilization of the respective differences in religiosity. Consequently, long-term stability in being a religionist or a nonbeliever will increase.

The affinities at this age between religiosity and generativity, or at least specific ways to exert it, can be noted through some meaningful trends. First, religious adults tend to favor fertility and parental investment in offspring. Compared to the nonbelievers, religionists of all major world religions and across continents, except Buddhists in some cases, desire and have more children – Muslims have the highest fertility rates. Religionists also tend to report high investment of their resources in parenting. Second, religious adults tend to highly endorse work ethic, i.e. considering work as an important value, as an end in itself, and as an important means for a successful life. This orientation, called by Max Weber "the Protestant work ethic," extends, in fact, to many other religious cultural contexts, beyond the traditionally Protestant ones.[30]

MIDDLE AND LATE ADULTHOOD: RECONSIDERING LIFE AND FACING THE PERSPECTIVE OF ITS END

The years of the so-called midlife crisis, as well as the years around retirement constitute opportunities for the reconsideration of one's own previous part of life and the undertaking of possible new initiatives for the re-orientation and re-examination of priorities. In terms of Erikson's theory, these challenges imply the developmental task of *integration*. These two moments thus have the potential to become pivotal for religious and spiritual change, in favor of either faith and practice or nonbelief and secularism.

Late adulthood, a period that has become increasingly longer today, conveys the perspective of cognitive and physical decline, the restriction of one's own social network, and the imminence of life's end. The first factor may restrict the elder's (public) religious practice, but the other two factors may facilitate intensification of religious belief. Nevertheless, the idea of late adulthood provoking people to become more religious needs to be nuanced.[31]

First, the difference between religious old adults and less religious younger adults is amplified by a cohort effect: older Western adults were born and grew up in more religious and less secularized societies. Second, beyond this cohort effect, longitudinal studies indeed favor the idea that older adults become more religious in belief and/or practice. This may be due to their greater time availability compared to previous ages, the need for social contact and support in an age of restriction of one's own social network, and the resurgence of existential questions and concerns. This trend, from the age of mid-60s and beyond, of an increase in religiosity, implies rather organized religion in some cultures, whereas in other cultures it implies personal faith. Interestingly, it is the very religious, in their combination of faith and practice, as well as the nonbelievers, who seem to have lesser fear of death, compared to the moderately or inconsistently religious who seem more fearful. Also, Christian and Muslim men, though, as shown in Chapter 2, believing less in God than women, are rather similar to women in the endorsement of belief in heaven and hell.[32]

Third, this pattern, even if significant, constitutes however only one possibility. As longitudinal and retrospective studies suggest, in addition to the increase, one can also observe a pattern of decrease in religiosity and spirituality during middle and late adulthood. People may also mature in the pathway of irreligiosity and/or feel freer from social constraints and thus distance themselves from tradition at a later age. Again, the other two trajectories of stability and continuity in religion or irreligion are well present.

It turns out that, contrary to the older idea of a unidirectional life span of religious development, aging allows for the diversification of trajectories with regard to faith, practice, spirituality, and religious belonging. The old models of the psychology of religious development we referred to in the beginning of this chapter, though pertinent to describe the trajectory of those who progressively become more mature in their faith, in line with normative liberal Protestantism, are far from providing us a picture that encompasses all trajectories. Importantly, these models neglect the possibility of similar developmental trends toward more abstract, symbolic, autonomous, and relativistic forms of the opposite attitudes, i.e. those of nonbelief and atheism.

CONCLUSION

The findings of the research we visited in this chapter indicate that our stereotypes regarding religion and human development may be imprecise and incomplete, and thus misleading. There is no evidence to conclude that children are naturally inclined to believe in a supreme being and that humans are oriented to spirituality as the answer to existential questions. But neither is there evidence to conclude that religious socialization violates the psychic world of an otherwise atheist child and that the cognitive development of humans as they grow will necessarily help them to realize the irrationality and unnaturalness of religion. To better understand the links between religion and human development, one has to perceive religion not only as believing, but also as bonding, behaving, and belonging.

Instead, recent research shows that children, though at the beginning, as early preschoolers, are rather skeptical toward invisible elements, they become progressively receptive of religious beliefs and rituals if adults present these beliefs and rituals as credible and efficient. Except for detrimental religious forms and experiences (cults, fundamentalism, abusive clergy), religious beliefs and rituals, in particular prayer, are generally welcome by children as fitting within their cognitive, emotional, and relational world. The religious elements involve some universal beliefs (intentionality behind things, body-soul dualism), the theory of mind capacity, curiosity and imagination for limited counterintuitive elements, wishful thinking, awe in the face of majesty, trust of specific loving others, and the emergence of cultural identity.

Religious socialization, and very likely irreligious socialization too, are more successful, i.e. remain stable across the life span, in the context of positive family relationships and broader societal normativity of, respectively, religion or secularism. Beyond this considerable stability, the developmental changes during different age periods may result in various religious changes.

Doubting, questing, and possibly abandoning religion, primarily its institutional aspects but also religion as belief, can occur at all age periods, but in particular in adolescence and early adulthood. These ages involve major changes in the physiological, cognitive, emotional, social, and moral domains that orient adolescents and young adults toward exploration, individuation, and search for coherence at a more abstract level, as they work on two major developmental tasks: identity formation and sexual mating, both of which facilitate religious distance. Overall, religion at this age period implies commitment to identity, and not necessarily exploration, as well as restrictive rather than permissive sexuality. For religious youth, religion becomes a factor of self-control and stability more than of plasticity and exploration.

Inversely, though to a lesser extent, transforming, (re)discovering, or intensifying faith, practice, and religious identity can also occur at all age stages, including emerging adulthood, but in particular in two moments. First, religiosity may increase during family formation: the developmental task of generativity implies at that period the willingness to transmit values and culture and help the young to grow. Second, late adulthood may increase religious and spiritual needs and interests as part of the developmental task of integration of one's own life into a meaningful whole and the reconsideration of existential questions as life's end approaches. These changes in favor of increased religiosity have a good chance to follow a developmental maturational pathway, with faith becoming more symbolic, spiritual, integrated, and flexible, but they may also result in transformation toward more radicalized forms.

Overall, beyond the possibility of peaks against or in favor of religion at some age periods, life span development relative to religion and spirituality becomes in adulthood less unidirectional and increasingly diverse and multidirectional. Finally, in normatively secular societies, where the development of those socialized as atheists is rather new and thus understudied for the moment, one may presume that similar maturation trends should apply to nonbelief across the life span – including the possibility of being interested in religion due to exploration and other developmental forces.

4

DOES RELIGION MAKE US MORE MORAL?

In many countries, including secularized ones, a major justification of the public acceptance and financial support of religious institutions, including schools, is the belief that religious teachings strengthen citizens' values and morality. A second justification is that religion contributes to people's sense of meaning, identity, and life goals, and thus to their well-being. Is this the case? Nonbelievers typically doubt this and may even think that religion is irrelevant or detrimental to morality and well-being. For them, religious believers are no more moral than are atheists, and may, rather, be moral hypocrites. Similarly, nonbelievers think that believers are just subjectively convinced they are happy. We will examine the religion-morality connection in this chapter and the religion-health connection in the next one.

RELIGION DOES NOT CREATE BUT ORIENTS MORALITY

RELIGION AND CHILDREN'S MORALITY

In the beginning of the 20th century, Freud argued that children acquire a sense of morality only when, at the age of four to five years, they internalize the paternal figure, which becomes the basis of the individual's superego, the instance englobing inhibitions, rules, and norms. In the mid-20th century, Piaget also thought that children are heteronomous – they only follow what parental, educational, and other authorities present as good or bad – becoming progressively autonomous in adolescence. In line with these theoretical perspectives, one is tempted to assume that religion plays the role of an authority that constitutes a source, if not a foundation, of morality in people's lives, and through parents, in children's lives.

However, original work by Elliot Turiel in the 1980s indicated that children do not wait for parental or other authorities' moral teachings to develop a sense of what is good and bad. As early as three years of age, children have a sense of the value of care/no harm as well as of fairness and individuals' rights, and they can criticize parents or religion for not being moral. These principles of care/no harm, fairness, and rights seem to be universal across cultures. From that perspective, religion does not create morality, but religious norms may parallel and boost some moral principles, or oppose and fragilize them, or rather selectively orient people to hold certain moral preferences. Religious ideologies provide micro-theories that orient people's decisions and value priorities, especially when facing complex moral choices. For instance, both pro-life and pro-choice supporters consider human life and individual freedom to be important values; but religion provides an ideology that specifies how we should define the human person and what the hierarchy between individual freedom and sacred values should be.[1]

RELIGION AND MORALITY: CONNECTIONS, INDEPENDENCE, AND CONFLICT

Consequently, rather than believing that religion creates morality and that without God everything is permitted, it is more accurate to consider that humans have a natural inclination to distinguish between right and wrong. As we will see in this chapter, religion promotes and, to some extent, effectively boosts important aspects of universal morality, mainly care for others and compassion – religious charity and volunteering being typical illustrative examples of this across history. However, religion also shapes morality by orienting it in certain directions. It does so first by "extending" the moral domain to additional norms beyond just universal values (e.g. sexual or ethnoreligious purity, conformity to tradition), and second by promoting a specific hierarchy between values – see Abraham's obedience to God asking him to sacrifice his son. Moreover, for believers, religiousness implies the need and willingness to be, and to be perceived by oneself and others as, moral and/or religiously righteous, which includes the need to have consistency between one's own values and acts.

Nevertheless, the discrepancy in the religious sphere between values and acts creates room for what is known as religious moral hypocrisy – the scandal of clerical sexual abuse indirectly facilitated by specific religious ideas and practices is a prominent example. Moreover, conflict between moral and religious norms, or priorities given to some values over others, may lead to decisions and acts that several others could perceive to be immoral (e.g. raising one's children within a sect disconnected from the broader society), or that are universally considered immoral, such as killing heretics for the salvation of their souls or killing innocents to propagate religious goals.

In this chapter, we will examine the empirical evidence on the links between religion and morality organized into three sections. These will focus on the role of religion with regard to: first, care for others and prosociality; second, other aspects of morality, mainly those oriented toward self-control and order; and finally, moral opposition, hostility, and immorality, partly as a consequence of religious priorities between diverging norms.[2]

RELIGIOUS PROSOCIALITY: LIMITED BUT REAL

Many of the classic theorists in the beginning of the 20th century, but also contemporary theorists in evolutionary psychology, converge on the idea that religion has contributed, and possibly still contributes, to human cooperation, care for others, and social cohesion. Across theories, the explanations may vary, but the directions of the conclusions are similar.

According to these theorists, religion, as it is intrinsically interwoven with culture, has norms that limit natural aggressiveness and egotism (Freud) and foster moral behavior through specific reinforcements and punishments, like the belief in heaven and hell (Skinner). In addition, religion makes altruism, though at first glance costly, conceivable and effective through the examples of saints demonstrating charity (James), and plays a particular role in motivating generativity as a developmental task central in adulthood (Erikson). Furthermore, religion consolidates society's coherence through shared beliefs and practices (Durkheim), and broadens natural (genetic, geographical) frontiers of kinship, to which natural altruism applies, to larger cultural kinships and coalitions (world religions) to which an extended altruism applies (Daniel Batson, Lee Kirkpatrick). Finally, religion has allowed for the historical transition from small communities with strict social moral control to large societies where an omniscient God observes and punishes immoral acts that would otherwise remain hidden and anonymous (Dominique Johnson, Ara Norenzayan).

What does the empirical research show us today? Does religion indeed enhance altruism? Are religious believers to some extent more prosocial than nonbelievers? If yes, how? If not, why?

PRIMING RELIGIOUS IDEAS

Two seminal sets of studies showed that participants, Canadians and Belgians, who were subtly exposed, beyond their conscious cognitive control, to religious words were quicker to identify words related to altruism, took more flyers to distribute for a charity, and shared to a greater extent hypothetical gains with others. In other words, religious ideas "automatically" activated an accessibility of prosocial ideas and behaviors of generosity and cooperation.[3] Since then, dozens of similar studies have been conducted across various cultural and religious contexts, both Western and non-Western. Though not always replicable, when results are significant, they consistently show that implicitly presented religious ideas, images, or symbols activate prosocial intentions and behavior. The effects are clearer for religious believers, but some studies indicate that the implicit religion-prosociality association in people's minds may also exist among nonbelievers.[4]

Of course, this does not mean that only religion is capable of implicitly activating prosociality, that it does so beyond any psychological explanation, or that the activated motivation of the prosocial orientation is necessarily altruistic. Studies indicate that the effects of religious priming on prosociality can be explained by the power that religious ideas and symbols have in activating empathy and oneness with others, but also in activating the need for conformity, or the need for a positive self-image. Moreover, nonreligious authority and nonreligious reinforcements or punishments can also activate prosocial intentions or behaviors. Finally, ideas that reflect the devotional dimension of religion (e.g. the belief in God) seem to be more efficient at activating prosociality, compared to ideas that reflect coalitional, i.e. institutional and group-oriented, religion.

PROSOCIALITY OF RELIGIOUS BELIEVERS

A partly different question is whether religious believers differ from nonbelievers on prosociality. There is substantial evidence that religious people are characterized by stronger prosocial orientation than nonbelievers, with this being attested to in their *self-reported* values (care, benevolence), emotions (empathy, gratitude, compassion), and various forms of prosocial behavior such as low aggression, helping, forgiving, volunteering, and donating – including to nonreligious organizations. This is consistently found across different forms of religiosity, including fundamentalism, as well as across religions, with some interesting differences in the strength of the effect between denominations or religions. It is also found consistently across ages, with stronger prosocial orientation being already observable among religious adolescents and children, and finally, across cultures, with self-reported prosociality as a function of religiosity being stronger in modern secular countries compared to traditional religious ones, a finding that can possibly be explained by the more intrinsic motivation of religiosity in secular cultures.[5]

However, skepticism has been expressed as to whether the previously mentioned pattern of findings may reflect (1) religious people's need for a positive self-image rather than a real concern for others' well-being and (2) merely the self-perception of believers as being prosocial but not actual prosocial behavior, that is, acts that benefit others. Experimental work by Batson in the 1980s and early 1990s, carried out exclusively with young US adults, indeed indicated that people who are more religious are no more helpful than less religious people, unless self-presentation concerns have been aroused.[6] More radical criticisms have questioned any effect of religion on prosociality for various theoretical and methodological reasons, suggesting that any and all connections between religion and prosociality seem to be only in people's minds.[7]

In an initial theorization and set of studies in my laboratory, we suggested that the question of the altruistic versus self-interested quality of the prosocial *motivation* among the religious is different from the question of the presence and the extent of prosocial *behavior* among them. We also suggested that religious prosocial behavior is not restricted to self-perceptions and is not a pure artifact of social desirability. It is *real*, that is, quantitatively more present among believers than nonbelievers and attestable from the evaluations given by others and through behavioral indicators. However, it is *minimal*, more easily observable in the everyday life rather than in highly sacrificial behavior, and typically *limited* to ingroup members but not really extended to unknown people and outgroup members; only modern, non-necessarily religious spirituality should imply universal altruism. In a later theorization, I also argued that *nonbelievers'* prosociality, even if quantitatively less present, should be more intrinsic in its motivation and universalistic in its scope, thus able to overcome ingroup/outgroup barriers. Additionally, I have argued that religious prosociality should be *compassionate*, i.e. more clearly observable when the target is in need and less clear when the study's participant is expected to simply share hypothetical gains with others in lab experiments. Finally, religious prosociality is *conditional*, that is, in order to be observed, it must not conflict with other competing religious moral principles (e.g. purity, honesty, just-world beliefs).[8]

Numerous studies conducted over the last 15 years across countries and various religious contexts have provided an overall confirmation of the previously mentioned. In studies that provided significant results, religiosity is usually found to imply prosocial *behavior*.[9] This translates into the perception of religious people by others, not only their friends but also their colleagues, as prosocial. It includes low aggression as a response to a frustration test and low use of hostile humor, as well as greater trust, physical closeness and cooperation measured in the lab, costly behavioral acceptance to volunteer and help, spontaneous sharing of hypothetical gains with proximal others and charity organizations, and making life choices for study fields and respective job domains that imply care for others, such as education and health.

Moreover, as anticipated, religious prosociality is compassionate – it implies helping a child when in need, but not when not in need – but is not unlimited. Religious people are ready to help proximal targets and ingroup members in need, but not unknown targets or moral outgroups (e.g. a gay person, a single mother, a feminist) with the same need. They also demonstrate spontaneous offers to help a student simulating a broken leg if that student is of the same religion, but not if s/he is of a different religion. Finally, religious prosociality toward the needy is not so profound and generalized: it is better activated when the religious norms and, more generally, a religious "mindset" become salient, e.g. after reading a relevant biblical text, in front of a religious building, or on Sundays or religious holidays rather than weekdays.[10]

COMPETING PRINCIPLES, MORALIZATION, AND SELF-CONTROL

Beyond common explanations of why people are not always prosocial (e.g. it is costly), part of the limitations of religious prosociality comes from the fact that religion also promotes other values, in addition to the universal values of care and justice that are at the heart of inter-personal morality. Some qualify this as an "extension" of morality to other domains, pointing for instance to our duties to the self, to the (in)group and society, and possibly to God and/or a more abstract sacred and moral order of things in the world. Note, though, that speaking of "extended morality" may be misleading, since these addi-tional values are not universally considered to be moral (e.g. respect for authority), and that some of their consequences may be immoral, such as symbolic or real aggression toward moral outgroups through submission to authority.

RELIGION AND "EXTENDED" – MOSTLY RESTRICTIVE – MORALITY

There has been substantial research on the relationships between religiosity and values and moral principles, organized into models varying across theorists. These models mainly include (1) Shalom Schwartz's model of values, (2) Jonathan Haidt's model of moral foundations, (3) Elliot Turiel's model of sociomoral domains, and (4) several two-dimensional models that distinguish between deonto-logical/normative morality and consequentialist/utilitarian morality.

VALUES AND MORAL FOUNDATIONS

Schwartz and collaborators, starting in the 1990s, established the existence, across countries and continents, of ten *values*, i.e. goals that people find important and that motivate their actions. Individuals and groups differ, however, in the priority they give to these differ-ent values. The ten values, integrated into two bipolar axes, include: tradition, conformity, and security (values denoting conservation), which oppose self-direction (autonomy) and stimulation (values denoting openness to change); as well as benevolence and univer-salism (denoting self-transcendence), which oppose achievement, power, and hedonism (denoting self-enhancement). Across genders, ages, countries, and religions, particularly the three monotheisms, religious people typically attribute high importance to conservation, especially tradition, and lower importance to openness to change, especially self-direction. They also attribute high importance to benevolence, and low importance to hedonism. Open-minded religiosity and modern spirituality accentuate the priority of the values of self-transcendence, particularly universalism, over the values of self-enhancement.[11]

More recently, in the late 2000s, Haidt and collaborators developed a theory on five principles, called *moral foundations*, organized into two sets. The first set of foundations, called "individualizing," denotes respect for all individuals and includes care for others/no harm and fairness. These two foundations are universally valued, across individuals and societies – see also the early theories on moral development by Lawrence Kohlberg and by Carol Gilligan defining, respectively, justice and care as universal values. The second set of moral foundations, called "biding," denotes how people are bided into groups and societies, and includes respect for authority, loyalty to the ingroup, and purity toward the sacred and moral order of the world. These three foundations are valued by conservatives and are important in collectivistic traditional societies. Several studies across various countries have shown that religiosity implies the endorsement of care to some extent, but also, and more importantly, the endorsement of collectivistic values, particularly purity.[12]

Taken together, the two research traditions using these two models show that religiosity, in addition to reflecting care for others, strongly reflects collectivistic moral concerns for social stability, conservation of tradition, and personal purity. This "extended" morality means that religion favors a *restrictive* morality: these values restrain openness to change and individual autonomy.

MORALIZATION AND DEONTOLOGY

Another way to describe this "extended" religious morality, which is in fact restrictive of flexibility, is to qualify this trend as high *moralization.* Turiel's theory and research on socio-moral judgment distinguishes between three domains: (1) the strictly moral domain of universal values, that is no harm, justice, and individual rights; (2) the conventional domain where norms depend on social conventions (e.g. calling parents by their first names or not); and (3) the personal domain, in which decisions depend on personal preferences (e.g. how to dress). Conservative religious groups such as the Amish, Orthodox Jews, and members of small-sized new religious movements have been found to be characterized by the tendency to moralize all decisional issues across all three domains, i.e. social, conventional, and personal.[13]

A final way to consider religious moralization is to examine the conflict between, on the one hand, deontological, rule-based, and principlistic moral reasoning and, on the other hand, consequentialist, empathy-based, and utilitarian moral reasoning. For instance, will I visit my friend in the hospital because I empathize with his/her situation or because I must obey a reciprocity norm? Can I lie or steal something to save somebody's, including a loved one's, life? A series of recent studies of monotheistic traditions across countries suggests that religiosity typically implies a preference of deontology over consequentialism.[14] Nevertheless, when the detrimental, antisocial, consequences of deontology seem high, religionists' care/empathy may contest the impact of deontological thinking.[15]

A SELF-CONTROL-ORIENTED MORALITY

Another way to describe religious morality is that, in addition to care for others, or perhaps above all, it aims to foster personal control. Self-mastery has been praised as a central ideal across religions and spiritualities in human history. In its intense form, this ideal characterizes the very nature of religious asceticism, that is, the effort, through heavy investment in everyday practice, to influence body and mind by controlling the content and spiritual quality of one's own thoughts, affects, and behaviors. In the old monastic Christian tradition, this included even managing the content and the influence of phenomena that escape from our conscious control, such as desires, dreams, and laughter. The ideal of self-mastery is also the common feature, a sort of global "moral muscle," behind the seven capital vices and corresponding virtues.[16] In its pathological form, religious self-control becomes, as we will see in Chapter 5, the central feature behind religious obsession.

The capacity of religious elements to foster self-control in the everyday life is confirmed in contemporary psychological research, at least as far as monotheistic contexts are concerned. It has been argued, and found, that the connection between religion and moral order is clearer in those contexts because monotheisms have developed and consolidated the idea of a personal God who is the guarantor of moral order.[17] Experimental research has shown that subtle exposure to religious ideas, beyond participants' conscious control, diminishes impulsivity, increases participants' endurance and resistance to temptations, and boosts self-control, especially when the latter has been threatened and there are no alternative resources to compensate for it. Moreover, there is substantial cross-cultural evidence that religious people tend to consume less alcohol, tobacco, and drugs. Emerging research also suggests that religious shoppers are more careful when buying, tend to spend less money in grocery stores, and prefer diet-oriented foods.[18]

The strong connection between religion and moral and social order translates into implicit associations in people's minds with a spatial representation of verticality in which up represents God/religion and morality, and down corresponds to the devil and immorality. A social and moral embodied map of beings implies a hierarchy that starts from the highest level (with God, who is supra-humanized) and goes through intermediate beings (angels, holy figures, men, and then women), to lower levels (outgroups, which are infra-humanized, animals, and demons). Such a hierarchy enhances the sense of order in one's own internal world.[19]

MORAL OPPOSITION, HOSTILITY, AND PREJUDICE

Moral concerns for self-control, order, and conservation, in addition to those for care, may explain the fact that religious prosociality is conditional: it is potentially inhibited, or may even be replaced by, hostility when believers are confronted with competing religious/ moral principles. We will examine this situation next by focusing first on strictly moral issues and moral outgroups, and second on ethnoreligious outgroups and prejudice.

MORAL OPPOSITION AND HOSTILITY

Religious prosociality not only does not extend, as we have seen, to include moral outgroups as beneficiaries of help, but may also predict a low willingness to help, or even hostility against, people who are perceived to threaten religious values (e.g. sexual minorities). Closed-minded forms of religiosity such as orthodoxy or fundamentalism imply a belief in the so-called *immanent* justice (people get what they deserve) and consequently a low willingness to help unemployed or homeless people, especially when the latter are perceived to adhere to an immoral way of life, and thus deemed responsible for their situation. On the contrary, belief in the so-called *ultimate* justice, i.e. justice will be found at some point in human history or in the afterlife, helps symbolic believers to act prosocially in favor of such people in need.[20]

There is also evidence that personal religiosity, particularly fundamentalism, is positively related to all three components of authoritarianism, i.e. socio-moral conservatism, submission to the established authorities, but also authoritarian aggression. Fundamentalist religiosity, holding a negative image of God, and sometimes even religious attendance, may be related to the endorsement of capital punishment and justification of violence. On the contrary, holding a positive image of God and devotional aspects of religiosity (e.g. prayer) can imply the opposite, i.e. compassion.[21]

Religious people typically report valuing and practicing forgiveness in general. Moreover, exposure to religious primes, or exposure to humility primes among the religious, has been found to diminish retaliation. However, the links between religiosity and real forgiving behavior or the readiness to forgive specific transgressions are not yet established.[22] Concerns of how transgressions should be sanctioned may explain this discrepancy. For instance, in Islam, the acknowledgement by the offender of their fault is considered a necessary condition for forgiveness. Jews, unlike Protestants, do not necessarily consider all offenses to be forgivable by humans.[23] It may also be that religious people who endorse the belief in immanent justice favor some kind of retaliation, whereas low forgiveness is facilitated, among symbolic believers, by the belief in ultimate justice as previously defined.

Similarly, organ donation, a typical altruistic act, generally supported today by the major world religions, does not adhere to the generally positive religion–donation association.[24] This is possibly due to conflicting religious views having to do with purity and physical integrity. Moreover, a vertical representation of socio-moral order, with men being considered superior to women, and an interpretation of purity in patriarchal ideological terms, may explain why religiosity is usually associated with gender inequality across religions. This may also explain why subtle exposure to religious primes has been found to increase sexism, particularly benevolent sexism, in both the US and secular Europe among both men and women.[25]

There are also several moral issues that seem to create a struggle among religious people between concerns for care and concerns for collectivistic values, especially purity. The discourse of major world religions today toward homosexuality favors the "hate the sin/love the sinner" distinction. However, research across countries suggests that the endorsement of this distinction serves to legitimize religious antigay prejudice. Experimental research shows that religious people are unwilling to help gay targets, financially or otherwise, not only when the cause is "immoral" (pro-gay), but also when the cause is neutral or even noble (e.g. visiting one's grandmother).[26] Similarly, religious opposition to the liberalization of issues such as abortion, euthanasia, and gay adoption (i.e. giving people the legal possibility to make their own decision on these debatable issues) is often justified today by care-oriented arguments that emphasize the need to protect the weak: the unborn, children, and the elderly. However, such moral opposition has been found to be explained by the endorsement of collectivistic values that emphasize tradition and the group over individuals, and not by the endorsement of the moral foundations of care and fairness.[27]

ETHNORELIGIOUS PREJUDICE

Do religious people perceive people of other races/ethnicities, religions, and ideologies (atheists) as outgroup members and thus treat them with prejudice and discrimination? Or, on the contrary, does religiosity increase tolerance, serving as a buffer against our natural inclination to dislike and discriminate against outgroups and ideological opponents? This question appears to be primarily a social issue related to intergroup relations, but also has a moral flavor. Are religious attitudes toward ethnoreligious outgroups colored by the values of care and tolerance, or by fear for the conservation of social and moral order? The answer to this question is not straightforward. The aspects of religion involved, i.e. coalitional versus devotional, as well as special features of social and cultural context, play some moderating role in the religion-ethnoreligious prejudice links.

Overall, the global trend of extensive research accumulated across the last five decades is that religious people tend to show prejudicial attitudes and discriminatory behavior against ethnoreligious (including immigrant) and ideological outgroups. This can be interpreted as a consequence of religious ingroup favoritism being extended to outgroup derogation. In other words, as we have seen, religion extends the frontiers of natural kinships to create broader cultural kinships where care applies. However, a side effect of this trend is the strengthening of the ingroup/outgroup distinction and, to some extent, subsequent outgroup derogation.[28]

Ethnoreligious prejudice is typically explained in psychological research as resulting from two, mostly distinct, processes. The first is an order-based fear of the unknown, the perception of the out-group as a symbolic threat to our values, and authoritarian attitudes of conservatism, conformity to authority, and legitimized aggression. The second process is a self-interest-based disregard of competitors, a perception of the outgroup as a realistic threat to our resources, and an endorsement of the so-called social dominance ideology, i.e. the consideration that, in our competitive world, the stronger group can legitimately dominate the weaker.

It is the first mechanism, i.e. conservative fear, rather than the second, i.e. self-interested social dominance, that has typically been found across studies to explain religious prejudice and discrimination against ethnoreligious and ideological (atheist) outgroups.[29] Thus, religious prejudice is generally more defensive of a hypothetical social and moral order than it is self-sufficiently offensive toward weak competitors to exterminate. This may help to understand that, though common religiosity across the world, despite cultural varia-bility, generally implies some political preference for the right-wing, and primarily socio-moral, not necessarily economic, conservatism, it also constitutes a restraint from endorsing extreme right-wing ide-ologies and parties.[30]

Nevertheless, the strength of the link between religiosity and authoritarian conservatism varies considerably across contexts. It is mostly moderately positive but can also be very strong or very weak. This helps us to understand important nuances in the previously mentioned pattern of research. In fact, the more authoritarian and coalitional a religion is, the more religiosity is accompanied by eth-noreligious prejudice. On the contrary, more devotional and spiritual faith implies less prejudice and, in some contexts, it may also trans-late into the tolerance of ethnoreligious outgroups. For instance, religiosity in secular Western countries has sometimes been found to predict low Islamophobia and a strong acceptance of multicultural-ism.[31] Finally, there seems to exist a notable West-East difference, with religiosity in monotheistic contexts contributing to ethnoreligious prejudice, but in Eastern Asian, particularly Buddhist, contexts contributing to ethnoreligious tolerance. Respective high versus low intolerance of contradiction partly explains this difference.[32]

Conformity to (divine) authority may be responsible of diverging effects. For instance, the positive association between religiosity and racism found in the US up to the 1980s diminished or disappeared afterwards once societal and religious authorities clearly and unambiguously portrayed racism as unethical and irreligious. Similarly, fundamentalists show outgroup hostility or, on the contrary, tolerance after reading a short biblical passage respectively justifying violence or praising love. Thus, religious prejudice is more evident when it is prescribed, and diminishes or extinguishes when it is proscribed.[33] Note that such religious proscription does not include sexual prejudice, which, as mentioned earlier in this chapter, is quite religiously legitimized. More generally, as shown in a recent set of original studies, religious people tend to use divine attributions to legitimize behaviors of questionable morality or passive immorality (e.g. keeping a lost wallet), but do not do so with active immorality (e.g. pickpocketing).[34] The same should thus be the case if we distinguish between prejudice with seemingly unclear (im)moral quality for the religious, and prejudice that is clearly perceived as immoral.

It would be unfair to close this section by addressing only outgroup prejudice shown by religious believers. What about atheists? Extensive research shows that, across the world, nonbelievers, compared to various kinds of religionists, are the lowest in prejudice against ethnoreligious and sexual outgroups and minorities. This is not surprising since nonbelievers also tend to be low on authoritarianism and socio-moral conservatism.[35] However, a very recent series of studies suggests that nonbelievers too, particularly atheists, have their own outgroups, i.e. ideological opponents against whom they may show prejudicial attitudes and discriminatory behavior (e.g. low willingness to have them as neighbors). Nonbelievers' ideological outgroups include those who threaten rationality and liberal values, i.e. fundamentalists and militant conservatives fighting against the legalization of abortion or gay rights, but also "mere" religionists of various major religions, including Buddhists who, compared to the Chinese, seem to be less liked by European atheists.[36]

CONCLUSION

Religion does not *create* morality in children's and adults' lives. Moral sentiment exists independently from religion, and several moral values are universal across cultures, but also across individuals, be they religious or not. However, religion *shapes* people's morality in various ways. The first is that religion enhances the universal morality of care and fairness and orients its applicability to several, though not all, targets. Second, religion complements this with less universal, social order-, self-control-, and purity-oriented values, thus generating restrictive morality. Religion also facilitates, to some extent, moral absolutism, but also moral rigidity, moral discrepancy between values and behavior, and deontological moral preferences with potentially antisocial immoral consequences. Finally, traditional religiosity goes hand in hand with conformity to (religious) norms and authority, which does not nourish autonomous morality and creates the risk of superiority of religious conviction over moral conviction.

Across individuals and across religious and cultural contexts, the more collectivistic and dogmatic a religion is, the more it places priority on the order-, self-control-, and purity-oriented dimensions over the prosocial dimension of morality. On the contrary, when religion focuses more strongly on its spiritual nature, care for others becomes salient, less restricted to the ingroup, and possibly extending to the ethnically, religiously, and morally different.

These conclusions, based on important research accumulated over the last decades, offer a more nuanced picture compared to many common ideas regarding the religion-(im)morality links. This research disconfirms or considerably qualifies common ideas that are often terribly diverging depending on personal ideological preferences. Key examples of such inaccurate ideas are: Without God everything is permitted; religion is socially useful since it fosters citizens' morality;

atheists are immoral or less moral than believers; religious people are moral hypocrites; and religion equally nourishes love and violence. In particular, regarding the latter, we have shown in this chapter that religion, on one hand, directly enhances prosociality, even if not universally. On the other hand, the non-prosocial or potentially immoral outcomes of religiosity (e.g. outgroup discrimination, moral de-responsibilization, legitimation of hostility, and non-consequentialist deontology) can be better understood as side effects of the subtle competition between religious and moral convictions, or between various diverging moral principles, rather than as being directly motivated by immoral dispositions and hateful inclinations.

Finally, the co-presence of care for others and self-control-oriented morality (certainly inhibitive and restrictive, but also to some extent proactive, in terms of competence to demonstrate and life goals to achieve), underlines and colors the moral attitudes and behaviors of religious people in several other life domains. These domains include, on one hand, sexuality, fertility, family, and parenting and, on the other hand, work, economy, and aspects of societal life implying civil responsibility such as honesty, attitudes toward democracy, pro-environmental values, and social action.

With regard to the first set of life domains, substantial empirical evidence, quite consistently across studies, cultures, and religions, favors the idea that religion has privileged the evolutionary strategy of adopting a restrictive sociosexuality: more restrictive and family-oriented, "hygienic" sexuality, with higher chances of investment in intra-marital fertility and attachment and investment of resources to children. Regarding the second set of life domains, the empirical evidence is more complex and diverse because of cultural, religious, and socioeconomic differences. Beyond valuing hard work, quality of relationships in the workplace, and integrity in one's obligations to society, religious people seem to struggle between concerns for the common good and compassion for the weak, on one hand, and conformity to, or the need to distance oneself from, traditional and conservative norms when it comes to moral issues related to the economy, democracy, social action, and pro-environmentalism, on the other hand.[37]

Does religion prioritize self-control-oriented "hygienic" morality over other-oriented morality? Several studies indicate that, overall, religion privileges the former. Nevertheless, studies focusing on cultural differences between traditional and modern societies suggest that things are about to change, with religious interpersonal morality possibly becoming a bit more salient in modern societies.

5

IS RELIGION GOOD FOR YOU?

Religion and health have a long history of strong interconnection that dates back to ancient times. For centuries, people have been visiting temples in search of healing. Illness, be it physical or mental, has been interpreted in traditional cultures as possibly being caused by supernatural agents who punish or test humans (God) or put them into temptation (Satan). Most miracles across religions involve the healing of human suffering – other miracles essentially highlight gods' power to act by overcoming natural laws, for instance by changing water into wine or by walking on water.

Given the development of medicine and other health-related fields like psychology, it is reasonable to assume that the role of religion in physical and mental health has become progressively less important. Similarly, the shift from salvation to happiness as being a primordial goal in life has very likely minimized the role of religion and spirituality compared to health-related professions. Nevertheless, given that today happiness is one of the most important goals people have, all human activities are evaluated by citizens and scientists partly in terms of their significance for well-being. The question thus remains: Is religion good for you?

The investigation of the relationships between religion and spirituality, on one hand, and physical and mental health (or psychopathology), on the other hand, has been the most prolific area of research in the field of psychology of religion. Many hundreds of studies and publications from the last decades, and more than a hundred reviews of that research within the last 15 years, attest to the scientific and social interest in these questions.[1] This interest is certainly genuine and intrinsic, but it may also be encouraged by personal motives. Proving that religion does or does not contribute to health and well-being could, respectively, provide value to religion or marginalize it. It goes without saying that the amount of psychological and personal value, or lack thereof, placed on religion is not reducible to religion's effects on health.

RELIGION, PSYCHOPATHOLOGY, AND NEGATIVE (MENTAL) HEALTH

Religion has been suspected to nourish psychopathology, especially through two major ways. The first consists of a non-accurate and altered perception of reality and thus a fragile connection to the world. The second consists of an excessive and fearful adhesion to a certain set of norms, mostly those related to purity, and thus a fragile connection with a nonautonomous self. In classic psychoanalytic terms, these two dynamics point respectively to psychotic and neurotic tendencies.

A VULNERABLE CONNECTION TO REALITY

The first dimension, that of a fragile perception of reality, points to aspects of mental vulnerability such as irrational thinking, schizotypy (mild levels of eccentric perception), delusions (false beliefs usually involving a misinterpretation), and dissociative experiences (e.g. depersonalization). In more intense forms, it can imply hallucinations (sensation in the absence of a relevant external stimulus), schizophrenia and other psychotic disorders, and dissociative disorders. Several religious beliefs, even "mild" ones, can be suspected to potentially nourish or inflate these aspects of mental vulnerability. Some examples of these beliefs are: God gave me a mission; God is so close to me that I can literally see and hear him; the apocalypse could be eminent; Satan may possess me.

Can we affirm that religion *causes* such mental vulnerability and disorders? Most of the evidence that has detailed some affinity between religion and trends indicating a problematic connection with reality comes from case studies of religious individuals and religious figures, especially mystics. It is beyond the scope of this chapter to discuss these cases. I do think though that it is important to make a point here. Part of this literature has been driven by the desire to show that individuals who have been perceived and venerated as saints were in fact suffering from psychopathology; or by the contrary desire to show that these figures were of healthy mind, thus truly holy and simply self-transcending.[2] This a priori opposition between sainthood and madness, or congruence between holy and healthy, is misleading. It is conceivable that some people may combine mental vulnerability and even illness with a life dedicated to a religious ideal. It has also been argued that some saints may have succeeded in transforming the dysfunctional aspects of their vulnerability, for instance pathological narcissism, into a constructive and creative aspect, for instance by founding a new successful religious order.[3]

Beyond these case studies on mystics and other religious figures, when focusing on the general population, studies show no evidence that religion causes schizophrenia and other psychotic and dissociative disorders, or that religious people are overrepresented in these diagnostic categories. Other research indicates that, for people suffering from schizophrenia, being religious may help them to cope. What is clear, however, is that religious themes are "appealing": when culturally available, they are often present in the psychotic ideas of people with preexisting psychopathology.[4]

Nevertheless, the findings mentioned earlier do not imply that religiosity is completely exempt from the potentially maladaptive tendency to inadequately perceive and connect with reality. An important body of studies indicates that religious people, or some types of them, are slightly prone to several cognitive biases (e.g. believing in body-mind dualism, life of the material world, purpose behind inanimate phenomena), magical thinking (the belief that one's own thoughts, wishes, or desires can influence the external world), some non-pathological schizotypal traits (e.g. extrasensory perception, the over-assumption of normally invalid causal links), and political and medical conspiracy beliefs. Also of interest to note is that people who are "spiritual but not religious" or high religious questers may be more inclined than traditional, mainstream, religious people to show an interest in and openness to unusual ideas, uncommon experiences, and alternative considerations of everyday reality.[5]

Finally, religiosity is often related to the endorsement of nonreligious paranormal beliefs. However, it is typically the mildly religious people who also endorse paranormal beliefs, whereas both atheists/skeptics and the very religious tend not to embrace such beliefs, even if for different reasons, i.e. strong rationality for the former, and competing worldviews for the latter. Highly religious people differ from paranormal believers in disposing of an internal locus of control ("I can have some control over my world") rather than an external locus ("My world is mostly influenced by external forces") and in their higher dispositions toward proximal others and order conservation.[6]

A FEARFUL SUBMISSION TO (PURITY) NORMS

Religious *beliefs and worldviews* are capable of sustaining misperceptions or an eccentric perception of reality when overinterpreting what we see or do not see, thus making religion attractive for the expression of *psychotic-like* tendencies. In addition, religious *practice and norms* have been suspected to sustain *neurotic-like* tendencies related to the fearful submission to rituals and rules and the repression of desires, particularly sexual ones. Freud has argued that religion is a sort of collective obsessional neurosis: religious rituals resemble obsessive repetitive acts aimed at repressing and canalizing our, mostly sexual, impulses.

Indeed, purification rituals are abundant across religions, and rites of religious passage emphasize the importance of abandoning the old "dirty" self to embrace a new "clean" self. Similarly, norms favoring restricted sexuality seem predominant across the major religious traditions. Holiness goes together with cleanliness, and excessive cleanliness indicates obsessionality. Note, though, that

Freud overemphasized the neurotic-obsessional dimension of religion. Many religious rituals, especially regular religious worship and prayer, have several other psychological functions, which are probably more central (see later in this chapter) than the hunt for purification and normative strictness.

OBSESSIONALITY

What does contemporary research tell us? Does religion cause obsessionality? Again, like for schizophrenia and psychotic disorders, the evidence favors the idea that people with a preexisting vulnerability for obsessive-compulsive disorders may find an appealing ground in religion to express their obsessive fears.[7] Going perhaps further, religion seems to offer a situation in which susceptible individuals can consolidate and find fuel for such tendencies. It does this through continuous demands for *orthopraxy*, in religious rituals and in everyday life behavior, and *orthodoxy*, in all or selected beliefs.

Many researchers and practitioners are familiar with the clinical category of *scrupulosity* as a special type of obsessive-compulsive disorder focused on religious and/or moral issues. For instance, people may constantly worry about performing rituals incorrectly, committing a sin, offending God, offending others, or acting ethically out of self-interest and not altruism. Nevertheless, research has not always been clear on whether religiosity is positively associated only with obsessionality as a personality disorder, which is a rather stable and not highly handicapping tendency for perfectionism and excessive concern for order and morality, or also with pathological obsessive-compulsive disorder. In the latter, patients are highly distressed by their obsessions, i.e. recurrent and persistent thoughts, urges or images the individual cannot ignore or suppress, and their compulsions, i.e. irrational and often ritualistic behaviors the individual cannot help but repeatedly perform hoping, in vain, to alleviate distress. Like schizotypy, which may be mild and non-pathological, or severe in the case of schizophrenia, obsessionality can be conceived as a continuum, ranging from mild vulnerability to psychopathology.

Research in recent years has made interesting advances in documenting the mechanisms behind the positive association between religiosity and obsessionality.[8] The stronger tendency of religious people, or certain kinds of them (Catholics seem more obsessional than Protestants and Jews; and Muslims more obsessional than Christians), to display obsessive-compulsive symptoms is explained by several maladaptive beliefs and affects. These include strong feelings of guilt, particularly sexual guilt, ideas of self-punishment, high sensitivity to disgust (particularly fear of contamination, sex, and death), perfectionism, an inflated sense of responsibility and an overestimation of threat, as well as a heightened importance given to the need to control one's thoughts. This latter importance is fueled by the belief in moral thought-action fusion, i.e. considering that simply thinking about an action is equivalent to actually carrying out that action, and that thinking about an unwanted event makes it more likely that this event will occur.[9]

SEXUAL REPRESSION

Sexual thoughts and affects are highly implicated in obsessiveness and moral and religious scrupulosity. This raises the question of whether religion and religiosity may have a negative impact on mental health through their emphasis on valuing restricted sociosexuality. At moderate levels, restricted sociosexuality reflects conservatism/ traditionalism, which is not detrimental to mental health. Furthermore, religion's restricted sociosexuality may have some positive influences on physical health through more "hygienic" and less risky sexual practices.[10] Nevertheless, excessive levels of restrictive sexuality may be detrimental for well-being through the repression of sexual thoughts, affects, and behaviors. In this case, sexuality is laced with guilt, disgust, fear of contamination and divine punishment, and ideologies of gender inequality.[11]

Studies suggest that these risks are present across cultural contexts. Religious Israeli adolescents may show compulsive sexual behavior when tending to suppress their sexual thoughts – what goes much further than simply acknowledging that sexual thoughts are not religiously normative. Similarly, among male Croatian adolescents with compulsive pornography use, it is the religious who increase their pornography use over time, despite having started with lower levels of pornography use than their nonreligious peers. Religious American men tend to perceive themselves as addicted to pornography even when their use of pornography is no higher than their nonreligious counterparts, and their use of pornography is related to low sexual satisfaction. More generally, religiosity, which is usually either unrelated or positively related to relational and marital satisfaction, is, however, often negatively related to sexual satisfaction.[12]

One should also note that, although religious themes are not particularly common in anorexia, there are indications in the family therapy literature of ethical codes of sacrifice, loyalty, and sexual denial in the families of anorexics. There also exist interdisciplinary studies on "holy anorexia," a religious valorization, in medieval and later ages, of very religious women, often reputed as saints, who practiced extreme fasting and self-denial.[13]

An alternative way to inhibit sexual thoughts is by their sublimation through art and creativity. Recent lab experiments show that Protestants excel in doing this.[14] However, immature and maladaptive forms of sexual restriction, fueled by normative religious ideas, seem to be partly responsible for the sexual abuse perpetrated by religious personnel having taken vows of chastity.[15] Importantly, most of these scandals involved hidden adult male to male, minor or adult, relationships. Thus, it is important to note here the detrimental effect of religiously justified covert or overt condemnation of nonheterosexual orientations, identities, and (sexual) lives. These religious prejudices constitute additional stressors that contribute to negative (mental) heath, especially among religious LGBT+ adolescents, young adults, and adults who experience strong conflict between their religious and sexual identities. More tolerant religious environments attenuate the previously mentioned effects.[16]

RELIGION, WELL-BEING, AND POSITIVE (MENTAL) HEALTH

In the previous part of this chapter, I examined how religion in general, or specific aspects of it, may facilitate the expression of mental vulnerability and possibly fuel the intensity of symptoms related to the maladaptive ways through which some people perceive and connect with reality (delusions, dissociation, eccentric thinking) and conform to norms that mostly denote purity, through obsessional ideas, compulsive acts, and sexual repression. In this second part, I will examine the role of general, common, religiosity (believing in God, religious attendance and prayer, self-identifying as religious and with a religious tradition) in average, nonclinical, people's quality of everyday life. As we will see, overall, the effect is positive. It is of modest size but covers several aspects of (mental) health, involves multiple psychological mechanisms, and is observable in many, though not all, societies.

WELL-BEING ACROSS SOCIETIES

In the last decade, studies analyzing large international data from many dozens of countries across the world, and with dozens or hundreds of thousands of participants, have painted both a global and nuanced picture of how religion relates to well-being. Does religiosity predict well-being and life satisfaction? Is the positive effect of religion the same at the individual level (religious people should be happier than their nonreligious peers) and at the collective level (religious countries should be happier than secular countries)? Do all major world religions similarly contribute to well-being? Are atheists disadvantaged compared to the religious?

Here are the big trends of the findings of these international studies and other studies focused in specific cultural contexts.[17] First, overall, across many if not most societies, there exists a modest positive effect, with (highly) religious people tending to be happier, more satisfied with their lives, and having better well-being and better psychological adjustment than nonbelievers and/or those who are weakly religious. Additionally, religiosity plays a buffering role by attenuating the detrimental effects that factors such as economic inequality or injustice have on happiness. Second, frequent religious attendance is often a better predictor of the previously mentioned compared to religious belief, possibly because the former combines the individual (belief in God's providence) and social (belonging to a supportive community) aspects that sustain the positive association between religion and well-being. Third, the effects generalize across men and women, but when differences arise, women seem to benefit more from religion. The effects also generalize across ages, though older ages seem to benefit more. Fourth, though there exist slight differences between the major world religions in the intensity of the effects and in the specific ways through which they contribute to mental health, overall, all religionists seem to benefit from their religion in terms of well-being.

Fifth, at the collective level, however, things go in the opposite direction. In more religious societies, people tend to be less happy, on average, compared to people in less religious or secular societies. This very likely reflects the fact that religious societies are also traditional societies of lower socioeconomic status, with important societal and health problems, thus often called "dysfunctional" societies, whereas secular countries are more "functional," with very positive socioeconomic indicators and far fewer societal and health problems. Of interest to note: a recent study suggests that it is a country's economy and not a country's mean religiosity that explains these national differences.[18]

This discrepancy between countries helps to understand another key finding that is recurrent across the international studies. The positive association between individual religiosity and individual life satisfaction is clear in the many countries that are religious, traditional, and also dysfunctional, but is less present or even inexistent in the fewer countries that are secularized, developed, and socially and economically functional. Several explanations, which are not incompatible but rather complementary, have been provided by researchers to explain the phenomenon.

First, in societies where religion is normative, being religious, which most often results from family socialization, is welcome and valued and helps people integrate well into the broader community: they swim along the stream. But, in countries where secularism is normative, or religion is no more normative than secularism, being religious is not valued, is not part of broad socialization, and does not particularly help people integrate into the global society: religious people swim against the stream. Second, in the religious and rather dysfunctional societies, people, and some certainly more than others, need religious beliefs, practice, and community to cope with significant problems such as economic inequality, poverty, weak or inexistent social security, and health and life insecurity. No such needs, at least not to such a critical degree, need to be compensated for by religion in the rich, developed, and rather secular countries, which typically offer personal and social security to citizens. Certainly, several people are religious in these secular countries too, but the primary psychological functions of their faith do not likely involve the search for existential security. Finally, nonbelievers may dispose of lower well-being in religious societies because nonbelievers in these societies constitute a minority and are potentially a target of distrust and discrimination. In secular societies, however, nonbelievers mostly come from nonreligious families, are not a minority, and thus do not differ from religious believers in terms of happiness.

SPECIFIC ASPECTS OF (MENTAL) HEALTH

The research mentioned earlier is based on self-evaluations of both life satisfaction and religiosity. One can thus be suspicious that religious people, who are known, as mentioned in a previous chapter, to be high in social desirability and provide answers to surveys in a way that could be seen favorably by others, may overestimate their level of subjective well-being. They may do so to give a positive impression to others ("You see: I am religious and thus happy") or to convince themselves by adopting a social stereotype or a religious norm ("I am religious, thus I cannot be but happy").

Certainly, believing that you are happy, even if not entirely accurate, is known to contribute to objective well-being and health. Nevertheless, examining more focused aspects of (mental) health and, when possible, some objective indicators, is one way to control for, and at least attenuate, the noise produced by social desirability in measures of self-reported subjective well-being. Additionally, longitudinal studies provide evidence regarding the direction of the effects: Is it religiosity that sustains health over time, or are healthy people more susceptible to becoming and remaining religious practitioners over time? Moreover, clinical trials provide an opportunity to verify causality. For instance, do spiritual interventions or the investment in religious practice contribute to health? Finally, lab experiments or real-life-based evidence allow for the identification of explanatory mechanisms: Does an increase of various kinds of threat to the self and well-being enhance one's attachment to God? Are religious people "immune," thanks to their faith, to these kinds of threats and thus do not respond to these threats in the same defensive way as nonbelievers?

Today many hundreds of studies provide detailed information on religiosity's role regarding specific aspects of health and mental health. This research is often based on self-reports; results are not always consistent; effect sizes are typically modest; and methodological weaknesses are not rare. Nevertheless, many studies are of good quality and there exist series of longitudinal, clinical, or experimental studies. These studies of different methodologies provide evidence that is converging and rule out the idea that everything regarding religious people's subjective well-being is simply a product of social desirability. Several domains of health, mental health, and well-being are concerned.[19]

Religion seems first to have some positive influence on diminishing *anxiety, loneliness,* and *depression.*[20] This points to religion's role in facilitating the *connection of the self with, and insertion into, the world,* especially when this connection has been rendered fragile. This is the case, for instance, following an illness of unclear cause and outcome, after the loss of a loved one, when mortality has become salient, and more generally when stressors in the everyday life or important traumatic experiences undermine well-being or create an existential threat. In line with this, some evidence suggests that religion's role in buffering stress is clearer among women, who are slightly higher than men in neuroticism, among older adults, and among ethnic minorities. In addition, very religious people tend to show slightly lower death anxiety compared to weakly religious people and seem immune to the usual effects of mortality salience in the lab. Finally, regarding depression, two directions seem plausible: religious attendance may offer protection from depression but becoming depressed may also diminish religious attendance.

Second, the studies favor the idea that religion also plays a protective role against mental health risks resulting from *impulsivity*, such *antisocial conduct* and *substance (ab)use*.[21] These effects seem to be rather broadly present across various cultures and religions. This points to religion's role in *facilitating self-control* and increasing it when threatened, a role that extends to less hostile, more *adaptive ways of interacting with others* and behaving in society. Alternatively, people with order-oriented personal dispositions and lower impulsivity – remember that the association between conscientiousness, low impulsivity, and religiosity is clearer in religious societies – may find, in religion, a worldview and way of life that solidify these tendencies, especially when these worldviews and ways of life are socially valued.

The two dynamics, i.e. insertion into the world and a more controlled relationship to the self and others, taken together may explain two additional effects of religiosity on more objective indicators of health, specifically, lower rates of *suicide* and suicidal attempts, and slightly higher *longevity*.[22] The effect regarding suicide (low rates and low suicide attempts, but not necessarily low suicide ideation) may be amplified by a possible lower propensity to report suicide as a cause of death in societies where it is still strongly condemned both religiously and socially. This possible bias, however, does not rule out the objective fact that religious people seem somehow better at managing despair. Of course, this pertains to religion in the general population, but there are indeed extreme cases of religious "suicide" for ideological reasons.

The effect regarding longevity, mostly attributable to religious attendance, is thin, with some additional religious people surviving compared to the nonreligious, or with religious people living on average few years more. It is, nevertheless, worth noting and very real: researchers have also observed this effect after having coded obituaries and gravestones. This effect, more clearly observable in religious societies, seems to be partly explained by hygienic practices such as low alcohol, drug, and tobacco use – but not lower obesity, which has unclear associations with religiosity. Orthodox religious groups seem to benefit from a slightly longer life, which can be partly explained by both the very strict hygienic ways of life and their high certainty in worldviews. Indeed, too many doubts and questions about existential, religious, and moral issues may be a sign of maturity but are often accompanied by anxiety and insecurity.

* * *

In conclusion, if we check the *Diagnostic and Statistical Manual of Mental Disorders* (DSM-V) categories, religion of the average religionist does not seem to be highly relevant in terms of having a positive or negative influence for aspects of mental health and psychopathology such as somatic symptoms, sleep-wake, bipolar, neurocognitive, and neurodevelopmental disorders, which are rather heavily dependent on biology and neurology. On the contrary, people's faith and practice seem to be involved to some extent in the way people *subjectively relate to the self, others, reality, and the world*. This includes obsessiveness, schizotypy, and dissociation, which have potentially positive affinities with some aspects and forms of religion, as well as anxiety, depression, traumatic stress, impulsiveness, antisocial conduct, and substance abuse, for which religion presents an overall buffering role.

EXPLANATORY PSYCHOLOGICAL MECHANISMS

What are the factors explaining the overall positive, even if modest, association between religiosity, well-being, and (mental) health? In this section, I will focus on the psychological mechanisms, which are cognitive, emotional, moral, social, and related to self-concept, and will link them to the four basic dimensions of religion: believing, bonding (through rituals), behaving (normatively), and belonging.[23]

UNIVERSAL MECHANISMS AND SPECIFICITY OF RELIGION

The psychological mechanisms that will be presented next play a universal role in the well-being and mental health of people in general, including nonbelievers and atheists. The latter can of course also be happy and benefit from the psychological factors contributing to well-being (e.g. social support for atheists organized into groups, optimism for secular humanists), and, as we have already seen, there are no remarkable differences in well-being between believers and nonbelievers in rich secular countries. There is also some indication that the association between religion and well-being is not fully linear, but partly curvilinear, with those who embrace a clear worldview, i.e. both the very religious and the convinced atheists, benefiting more than the weakly religious, the doubters, and the agnostics.[24]

The specificity of religion with regard to mental health is not any unique psychological mechanism, but the fact that religion offers a specific "package." For convinced and engaged religionists, this package consists of an integrated set of beliefs, rituals, norms, and a sense of community. This implies first that religion provides fertile ground for many of the diverse psychological mechanisms that contribute to well-being to flourish simultaneously, be they cognitive, emotional, moral, social, and/or those related to self-concept.[25]

Second, the four aspects of religion, i.e. beliefs, rituals, norms, and community, have additive influences that reinforce each other. For instance, religion promotes optimism, which is an interesting universal contributor to health. But it does so not only as (1) a moral ideal (secular humanists are also optimistic in their moral vision of the world), but also through (2) beliefs such the belief in immortality, (3) rituals, which esthetically, symbolically, affectively, and collectively galvanize optimism for a better future self and world, and (4) a community which perceives itself to be carrying out an eschatological dream (preparing and being part of a glorious new kingdom and a new world). A final specific way in which religion influences mental health is that it proves useful where alternative means and resources are lacking. This may be a lack at either the personal, dispositional level, which leaves some people needing religion more than others to feel better, or the contextual, situational level, in moments of important distress.

COGNITIVE, EMOTIONAL, MORAL, AND SOCIAL FACTORS

Figure 5.1 details the psychological factors that have been hypothesized and have – some occasionally, some repetitively – been at least partly found to explain the associations between religiosity and mental health. It has not yet been established in a solid and definitive way which factor(s) precisely explain(s) religion's influence on which aspects of mental health. We thus treat these factors as globally explaining religion's role on positive mental health and low negative mental health.

Of interest to note is that, if we take into consideration two of the major trends of existing research on religion and health showing that religious practice is the most powerful predictor among religious variables and that social support is the most important explanatory mechanism, we have to infer that religious rituals play a predominant role in mental health across religions. Very likely, the major religious rituals, i.e. regular public worship and prayer, along with other more focused rituals, facilitate the activation of most, if not all, the multiple and diverse mechanisms we will detail next.

Religious beliefs include primarily the belief in a providential transcendental entity, that is, in most world religions, a personal God perceived by most believers as both loving and powerful, thus combining maternal love and paternal protection, as well as the belief in afterlife and personal immortality, a belief important in alleviating death anxiety. (A small minority of believers have a negative image of God as punishing and malevolent, a concept that reflects neuroticism and

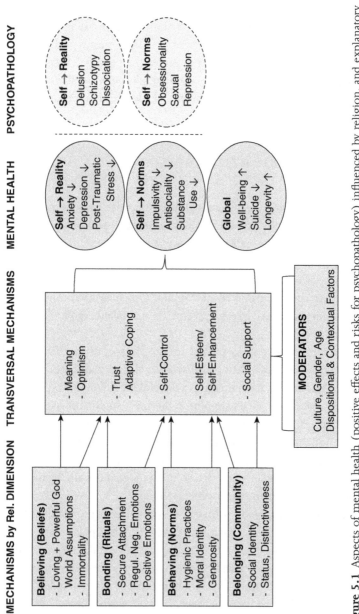

Figure 5.1 Aspects of mental health (positive effects and risks for psychopathology) influenced by religion, and explanatory psychological mechanisms, across and within the four basic dimensions of religiousness.

understandably translates into negative mental health.[26]) In addition, religious people tend to strongly endorse universal human beliefs known as basic "word assumptions." These beliefs are mainly that (1) the world and people are primarily benevolent, (2) there is some kind of justice in how things happen (we saw in Chapter 4 the concept of "just-world beliefs"), and (3) events are governed by some order, not randomness, and are thus controllable.[27] These universal beliefs are necessary for humans to function in everyday life and are fragilized following traumatic experiences. Note also that religious people, probably because they believe in the world and others' benevolence, are more trusting of others and are seen as trustworthy; nonbelievers tend to trust others less, even in secularized Europe.[28]

Religious rituals are very specific moments, most often taking place in designated spaces, where believers collectively or individually communicate with God, or another supernatural agent, who plays the role of a secure attachment figure to whom people communicate their thoughts and affects, ask for help or forgiveness, and/or express gratitude or, occasionally, dissatisfaction.[29] Moreover, religious rituals offer several means that allow for the regulation of negative emotions and affects such as sadness, fear, loneliness, anger, or guilt, by reinterpreting, minimizing, confronting, and/or esthetically and symbolically controlling and transforming these affects.[30]

Additionally, and perhaps most importantly, people across the world, for centuries, have regularly attended, mostly the same, religious services for the several positive emotions and affects they provide: inner peace, hope, joy, awe, inspiration, compassion, pride, and/or aesthetic beauty – but rarely or accidentally other positive emotions such as amusement or curiosity. Experiencing these affects collectively and ritualistically through music, symbols, synchronized movements, and conformity to a script amplifies the experience and its social and well-being-related effects.[31] This higher positivity in affects has been found to color the tweets of believers, compared to the tweets of nonbelievers, in an analysis of two million text messages of 16,000 users. It has also been found to distinguish US churchgoers from non-goers during both the week and Sunday, a day where churchgoers spend more time participating in pleasant activities shared with family members and friends.[32] Finally, beyond regular religious worship, there is a plethora of other religious rituals aiming to address concerns and celebrate affects related to specific life circumstances.

Religious moral preferences and norms, i.e. hierarchy between universal values and specific additional religious norms requesting orthopraxy, provide some additional contributors to mental health, but at the risk, as we have seen in cases of excessiveness, of fueling obsessive tendencies. Religiously endorsed order-, commitment-, and purity-oriented values, norms, and practices have some positive impact on health and mental health through the emphasis they place on some aspects of healthy lifestyles such as valuing work, low substance use, low risky sexual behavior, as well as the emphasis given to family values and investment in children. Religiosity thus seems to be, modestly but overall positively, related to relationship and marital satisfaction.[33] Additional contributors to well-being seem to be religion's valuing of moral identity, integrity, and coherence between values and acts, as well as prosocial behaviors of help, volunteering, and generosity: doing good for others is known, in return, to make us feel good.[34]

Religious community also contributes to religionists' well-being and (mental) health. Being part of the religious community helps satisfy the need to belong and provides a social identity that is exclusive – people belong to one religion, but may have several nationalities – and prestigious, since the community celebrates a glorious past and affirms a glorious future.[35] These offer status and distinctiveness, as we can see, for instance, by the importance religion holds among ethnic minorities and immigrants in maintaining distinctiveness from the national majority. Other research shows that, despite the religious ideal of humility, people need religion to self-enhance, that is, to consider themselves better than the average person and even better than the average co-religionist.[36] Furthermore, a key factor in explaining the religion-health link is the social support received thanks to the community.[37]

SELF-RELATED POSITIVE "ILLUSIONS" AND
POSITIVE COPING

Most if not all of the mechanisms mentioned earlier, boosted by the four dimensions of religion and religiosity, contribute, additively and interactively, to the enhancement of key aspects of self-concept known to be critical predictors of mental health and well-being. They have been characterized in clinical and social psychology as "*positive illusions*": meaning in life, optimism, self-esteem, and self-control. These four do not strictly correspond to accurate perceptions of reality. People overestimate both their capacity to control their world as well as their appreciation by their friends; and meaning and optimism are rather subjective, not objective, estimations. However, all these slight, not excessive, overestimations are more positive for mental health than the more accurate ideas ("I am an average person" and "I am not sure whether my life is meaningful and controllable"). Thus, religion's role in mental health can be seen as resulting from religionists' endorsement of such positive illusions: The world is a creation with a purpose; God considers me to be a unique and highly valued person; with God's help I will resolve this problem; at the end of this world, there will be justice and peace.

Finally, religion itself, i.e. several mainstream positive beliefs and practices, has been theorized and found to function as a coping strategy for stress. This is the case beyond several other coping strategies known to reflect either approach or avoidance of the problem and to be adaptive or maladaptive.[38] Beyond a vast literature on religious coping as a specific construct, other research has shown religious people's propensity to use some *coping strategies* and not using others. Across several religions and cultures, religiosity has been found to implicate a positive reframing/cognitive reappraisal of negative events, which is a clearly adaptive strategy, and the acceptance of unchangeable negative events, which in many cases is an adaptive strategy, and to be unrelated or negatively related to maladaptive strategies such as denial or avoidance. There is variability though across cultural contexts regarding religiosity's ability to predict the use of emotional expression or emotional suppression as a coping strategy.[39]

CONCLUSION

In its uncommon and worrying forms that suggest a vulnerable relationship with reality (delusional and depersonalized) or norms (obsessional and pleasure-repressive), religion seems to welcome, and potentially amplify, the expression of preexisting psychopathology through a selective focus on harmful relevant religious beliefs, norms, practices, or communities (e.g. cults). Nevertheless, even in this context, alternative, positive, religious sources of coping, if used, may help vulnerable individuals to attenuate the damaging effects of mental distress in everyday life.

When it comes to common religiosity of the general population, an important amount of research indicates that, overall, primarily frequent worship attendance, but also religious belief and identity, contribute, modestly – there are many other important sources of health and well-being – but broadly across domains, to subjective well-being, life satisfaction, and several aspects of mental and physical health. These aspects cover the two axes of the relationship of the self with reality and the world (low anxiety, depression, and loneliness) and with norms (low impulsivity, antisocial conduct, and substance use). Longitudinal, experimental, and clinical studies, and the use of more objective indicators, such as suicide rates and longevity, suggest that religion's effect on well-being is real, and not simply an artifact of religious people's positive self-perception. However, one must consider religion's contribution to well-being and health as being most often *compensatory* and *contextual*: it is stronger, or only evident, in groups with higher distress and in situations and cultural contexts where alternative resources for well-being and health are lacking, or where religion is socially normative.

The explanatory factors behind the positive association between religion and health are universal psychological mechanisms that, in the context of religion, are specifically facilitated by religious beliefs, rituals, norms, and a community, all of which reinforce each other. These are cognitive/existential (basic world assumptions, the belief in a providential transcendence, immortality as an answer to death anxiety), emotional/relational (trust, attachment security, regulation of negative emotions, some adaptive coping strategies, the experience of selected positive emotions), moral (hygienic practices, moral identity, care for others), and social (social support, social identity, and status/distinctiveness). Consequently, religion seems to enhance critical qualities of the self-concept: meaning, control, optimism, and self-enhancement, all known to be slightly "positive illusions" that contribute to (mental) health.

In summary, religion seems to not be, or at least to be less, relevant for disorders or aspects of health that are heavily influenced by biology. Religion is relevant, however, for the (un)healthy ways through which people subjectively relate to the self, others, the world, and reality. With the exception of few contexts where marginal negative religion attracts and potentially fuels vulnerability, overall, religious practice, but also belief and identity, as experienced by many religionists in most world countries, seems to constitute a modest but nonnegligible positive value for health and well-being. Finally, the fragility of religion may be the side effect of its force. Religion fosters meaning, optimism, self-esteem, and self-control, especially when these have been weakened, but the excessive distance from reality in the previously mentioned positive illusions may lead to overinterpretation and delusion, or to overcontrol and obsession.

6

WILL RELIGION SURVIVE?

Across the chapters of this introduction to the psychology of religion, we examined, based on accumulated and especially recent research, the psychological determinants and functions of religiosity at the personality, cognitive, emotional, moral, social, and life-span developmental levels. We saw religiosity's outcomes with respect to key life domains: self-concept, interpersonal relationships, intergroup relations, morality across various life domains, and health and well-being. We identified several universals in religion's psychological functioning but also noted interesting differences between cultures.

At the end of this "initiation," two intriguing and somehow interrelated questions arise. First, has religion been beneficial for humans? This question has, in recent years, been approached primarily from an evolutionary psychology perspective, that is: Has religion been adaptive for the evolutionary needs of the human species? Second, and in line with the previous question: Will religion persist? This question, which was central at the beginning of the 20th century when religion was considered a provisional intermediate stage in human development between magic and science, has come center again today but with the idea of religion's "return" or its replacement by nonreligious spirituality.

* * *

Most scholars today argue that religion may not have been, strictly speaking, necessary for the adaptive needs of the human species – these needs can be satisfied without religion. They nonetheless conclude that religion has been in line with, facilitating and not countering, these adaptive dynamics. Religion seems to have been useful for several important evolutionary psychological mechanisms, rather than only serving the motive of self-actualization, which is not an evolutionary need – humans could have succeeded in surviving without art or philosophy.

As we have seen throughout this book, these mechanisms include: (1) attachment to a caring and protecting (substitute) attachment figure; (2) preference for a restrictive, "hygienic," sociosexuality strategy favoring intra-marital fertility and investment in offspring; (3) building large coalitions through trust, reciprocity, and cooperation, facilitated by the belief in a moral supreme being controlling cheaters, a feature useful in big, anonymous societies; (4) inhibition of interpersonal aggression, but not of intergroup conflict, and consolidation of social conformity and submission to authority; and, (5) at the same time, individuals' acquisition of status and self-enhancement.[1]

As interesting and pertinent as these may be, they leave out our understanding of nonbelief and atheism, in terms of adaptiveness. How can it be understood that, although not socially valued or valued to a lesser degree, and despite being a minority, doubters and atheists have always been present across societies and human history? To answer this question, we need to complement the perspective mentioned earlier with an evolutionary understanding of individual differences, i.e. why there have always been believers and nonbelievers, and not only why religion has been predominant.

The explanation we can advance is that it is actually this variability between believers and nonbelievers that may have been adaptive, rather than religion alone or atheism alone. Nonbelievers and atheists bring contest, nonconformity, flexibility, creativity, analytic thinking and science, and thus change and growth, which are also essential for societies to adapt and develop. Thus, variability in religiousness can be evolutionarily understood like the variability in personality traits.

Highly agreeable people promote cooperation, whereas less agreeable people advance individual goals and interests even if it hurts others; each of these two orientations has its costs and benefits. Conscientious people accomplish goals following established standards, whereas people low in conscientiousness and high in openness to experience are indifferent to and defy these standards, and explore alternatives even when risky. At the group level, it is the variability within societies between those high and those low in a given trait that is adaptive: in some environments and moments, highly conscientious people are more needed, whereas in others, less conscious people become useful. Similarly, it is the diversity of having, within societies, believers and nonbelievers that may have been adaptive. In difficult environments hurt by economic inequality and severe threats, religiosity is advantageous. In functional societies that guarantee personal security and prosperity, irreligion becomes beneficial and attractive to make challenging scientific advances and explore and implement audacious changes.[2]

* * *

Will religion survive? On the one hand, the rapid secularization in the West gives some credit to several great thinkers of the early 20th century who predicted the end of religion thanks to the advance of modernity and science. Secularization has been rapidly increasing over the last 50 years in the West, leading to the point that major religious denominations in some Western countries are running out of candidates for religious ministry. Freud rightly predicted that, when social pressure falls, people will start abandoning religion. On the other hand, secularization has not been so spectacular as one could have predicted a century ago: about half of Europeans still believe in God or a self-transcendent entity. In addition, a vast majority of the world's population self-identifies with a religion; and some interpret today's manifestations of religious neoconservatism and radicalization as a return of religion.

The attempt to answer the question of religion's survival cannot be but interdisciplinary. I will, however, propose here some ideas from a psychological perspective. One possibility is that the evolutionary understanding of religious variability explained previously, with the co-presence of believers and nonbelievers within societies being adaptive, makes it very likely that religious believers and nonbelievers will continue to coexist, possibly for centuries. This could hold even if the mean level of religiosity in a given society or in the world continues to decrease as a function of secularization, or increases to some extent as a function of the higher fertility of the religious compared to the nonreligious.

Related to this is Freud's argument that the force of religion is rather the force of the needs and desires it seems to satisfy.[3] Certainly, these needs or motives for meaning, hope, control, self-esteem, belonging, and immortality – as we saw in Chapter 5, technically rather "positive illusions" – can also be satisfied within a nonreligious perspective. Nevertheless, religion's specificity is, as detailed in this book, the fact that religion addresses these needs through an integrated and coherent set of beliefs, rituals, norms, and community, each of which reinforces the other. In environments and moments pressing for high coherence between ideas, affects, values, and behavior, this becomes an advantage.

The limitation of this possibility is that it does not really integrate change, i.e. secularization. A second possibility, proposed by several sociology scholars, is that both secularization and religious zealotry will progress and end up to be antagonists producing increasing tensions in future societies between those holding secular liberal values and the religious bigots and fundamentalists. As indicated in Chapter 4, the current evidence is not strongly in favor of this. The major world religions, as history indicates, follow and adapt to, even if with inertia and delay, continuous societal changes. They do so possibly for intrinsic reasons, but certainly to survive; otherwise, they would marginalize and die. Thus, religionists in liberal societies have become less conservative, progressively sharing secular values. Many Western European Catholics are tolerant of those among their priests who live in a couple relationship, and many European Christians dislike fundamentalists and antiliberals almost as much as nonbelievers do.

Consequently, it will be only a small minority of religious radicals who will continue to oppose modernity. At the moment of writing this conclusion, i.e. early April 2020, only a thin minority of radicals across religions are opposing the temporary closing of churches, mosques, and synagogues in light of the global society's lockdown aimed at preserving numerous human lives from the coronavirus threat.

A third trajectory, which is my preference because it surpasses the previous two while integrating their value, is that, in addition to secularization, some variability between believers and nonbelievers will remain, but traditional religion will be progressively transformed into and replaced by modern spirituality – or to use another terminology, coalitional religion will weaken in favor of devotional religion. The psychological research we visited in this book suggests interesting similarities and differences between the two, or when shifting from the former (coalitional, traditional religion) to the latter (spirituality, devotional religion).

Overall, in modern spirituality, the traditional religion's emphasis on ideas, values, and practices denoting and favoring conformity, suspicion against autonomy, sexual inhibition, lack of relativism, and opposition to change is diminishing if not extinguishing – without however transmuting into an apotheosis of autonomy and a culture of change. In parallel, there is an increasing emphasis or re-centering on the importance of moral, emotional, and social self-transcendence. This is observable as a criticism of and discomfort with materialistic values, strict individualism, and pleasure as an end itself, and as an inclination for other-oriented and universalistic compassionate values and for experiencing self-transcendent positive emotions.

Will modern spirituality definitively become nonreligious or will it continue to have a religious flavor? This is more difficult to anticipate. As a psychologist observing religion, I would venture to guess that a fully nonreligious spirituality may have fewer psychological advantages and a lower positive cost-benefit ratio. Even if spirituality may be experienced independently of established, traditional, and well-structured religious institutions, it seems reasonable to assume that spiritual ideas, beliefs, affects, and values are reinforced by metaphors, symbols, legends, and role models situated in texts and other sources of religious traditions. Things are experienced more saliently as true, worthy and meaningful if they appear as not only rationally demonstrable and practically efficient, but also as being in line with, and to some extent validated by, some old wisdom. Finally, ideas, beliefs, and worldviews that are celebrated with relevant affects through some kind of ritual allow participants to reassure each other that the major concerns they share are true, worthy, and meaningful. This quasi-religious flavor may represent a critical feature distinguishing spirituality from secular humanism.

FURTHER READING

For mid-level authored books, see:

Why gods persist: A scientific approach to religion, 2nd ed., by R. A. Hinde (Routledge, 2010).

Psychological perspectives on religion and religiosity, by B. Beit-Hallahmi (Routledge, 2015).

Psychology, religion, and spirituality: Concepts and applications, by F. Watts (Cambridge University Press, 2017).

Invitation to the psychology of religion, 3rd ed., by R. F. Paloutzian (Guilford, 2017).

For larger multi-author and edited volumes and handbooks, see:

APA handbook of psychology, religion, and spirituality, 2 vols., ed. by K. I. Pargament (APA, 2013).

Handbook of the psychology of religion and spirituality, 2nd ed., ed. by R. F. Paloutzian & C. L. Park (Guilford, 2013).

Religion, personality, and social behavior, ed. by V. Saroglou (Psychology Press-Routledge, 2014).

Psychology of religion: An empirical approach, 5th ed., by R. W. Hood, P. C. Hill, & B. Spilka (Guilford, 2018).

The science of religion, spirituality, and existentialism, ed. by K. E. Vail & C. Routledge (Academic Press-Elsevier, 2020).

For books and overview texts on more specific themes, see references by chapter.

NOTES

CHAPTER 1

1 Pew Research Center (2017)
2 Saucier et al. (2015)
3 Saroglou (2011, 2014a)
4 Cohen et al. (2013)
5 Batson et al. (1993)
6 Saucier & Skrzypińska (2006), Zinnbauer & Pargament (2005)
7 Saroglou (2002a)
8 For fundamentalism, orthodoxy, religion-as-quest, and faith maturity, see respectively Rowatt et al. (2013), Duriez et al. (2007), Batson et al. (1993), and Fowler (1981)
9 James (1902/1985)
10 Pew Research Center (2017)
11 Saroglou & Cohen (2013); see also Norenzayan (2016) and Saroglou (2019)
12 For overviews of research methods, see Hood & Belzen (2013) and Saroglou (2014b); for the implicit measures, see Jong (2013) and Willard et al. (2016)

CHAPTER 2

1 Pew Research Center (2015, 2018a)
2 King & Boyatzis (2015); see also Copen & Silverstein (2008)

3 Hardy et al. (2011)

4 Nelsen (1990), Williams & Lawler (2001)

5 For parents' similarity on religion and politics rather than personality, see Ashton (2018)

6 Thiessen & Wilkins-Laflamme (2017)

7 Saroglou et al. (in press)

8 Kelley & De Graaf (1997), Müller et al. (2014)

9 Phalet et al. (2018), Rubin & Rubin (2014)

10 For this section on personality and religion, see, for reviews: Saroglou (2010, 2017)

11 Ashton & Lee (2019)

12 Gebauer et al. (2017a, 2018), Hermann & Fuller (2017)

13 Clobert & Saroglou (2015), Schwadel (2016)

14 For intelligence, see Cribari-Neto & Souza (2013), Zuckerman et al. (2013); for bullshit arguments, Erlandsson et al. (2018), Pennycook et al. (2015)

15 Webster & Duffy (2016)

16 Pennycook et al. (2016); see also Colzato et al. (2010)

17 Rosengren et al. (2000)

18 Wilson et al. (2014)

19 Boyer (2001)

20 Beit-Hallahmi (2015, ch. 5), Francis & Penny (2014), Voas et al. (2013)

21 Piedmont (1999), Zinnbauer & Pargament (2005)

22 Saroglou & Muñoz-García (2008), Saucier & Skrzypińska (2006), Willard & Norenzayan (2017); see also Gebauer et al. (2014)

23 Saroglou (2016)

24 James (1902/1985)

25 Exline (2013), Hui et al. (2018)

26 Saroglou (2010, 2017)

27 Jong & Halberstadt (2018)

28 Granqvist (2020)

29 See, for reviews, Laurin & Kay (2017), Sedikides & Gebauer (2014)

30 Saroglou et al. (2008), Valdesolo & Graham (2014), Van Cappellen et al. (2013)

CHAPTER 3

1 Oser et al. (2006), for a review

2 Barrett (2012), Heiphetz et al. (2016), Rosengren et al. (2000)

3   Boyer (2001), Talwar et al. (2011), Wigger (2019)

4   Norenzayan et al. (2006)

5   Busch et al. (2017), Evans & Lane (2011), Legare et al. (2012)

6   Heiphetz et al. (2016, 2018); but see Nyhof & Johnson (2017)

7   Harris et al. (2018) and Lane & Harris (2014), for reviews

8   Barrett (2012) and Lane & Harris (2014), for reviews; for Santa Claus as real, see Goldstein & Woolley (2016)

9   Freud (1927/1961); Saroglou (2006a), for a review

10 Granqvist (2020), for a review

11 Meuleman & Billiet (2011)

12 Boyer (2001), Demoulin et al. (2008), Leach et al. (2001)

13 Oser et al. (2006), for a review

14 Bamford & Lagattuta (2010), Lane et al. (2016)

15 Woolley (2000), Woolley & Phelps (2001)

16 Dunham et al. (2014), Heiphetz et al. (2013), van der Straten Waillet & Roskam (2012)

17 Hardman (2004), Nilsson (2016)

18 Buxant & Saroglou (2008), Mahoney (2010), Mahoney et al. (2001)

19 Gibbs & Goldbach (2015), Heiden-Rootes et al. (2019)

20 Böhm et al. (2014), Calkins et al. (2015), Harper & Perkins (2018)

21 Pew Research Center (2018b), Wink et al. (2019)

22 Saroglou (2012)

23 Good & Willoughby (2008), McNamara Barry & Abo-Zena (2014), Oser et al. (2006)

24 Lee et al. (2017)

25 Saroglou (2012), for a review

26 Saroglou (2019), for a review

27 Aalsma et al. (2013), Grubbs et al. (2017), Vasilenko & Lefkowitz (2014)

28 Wink et al. (2019)

29 Glick (2013)

30 Saroglou (2019), for a review

31 For this section, see Krause (2013) and Wink et al. (2019), for reviews

32 For the lack of a gender gap in these beliefs, see Pew Research Center (2016)

CHAPTER 4

1   Turiel & Neff (2000)

2   For this Chapter 4, see Saroglou (2019), for an extensive review

3 Pichon et al. (2007), Shariff & Norenzayan (2007)

4 Shariff et al. (2016), for a review; Saroglou (2019, p. 754, footnote 5) for new studies

5 Saroglou (2013, 2019), for reviews

6 Batson et al. (1993)

7 Galen (2012)

8 Saroglou et al. (2005), Saroglou (2012, 2013)

9 One study provided awkward findings, i.e. religious children were meaner, and received a large echo in the international media before finally being retracted because of inappropriate methodology: mixing of poor and rich cultures in the analyses

10 Saroglou (2013, 2019), Tsang et al. (2015), for reviews; see, in addition, Różycka-Tran (2017), Sabato & Kogut (2018), and Van Cappellen et al. (2017)

11 Roccas & Elster (2014), Saroglou & Muñoz-García (2008)

12 See several studies cited in Saroglou (2019, p. 735)

13 Nucci & Turiel (1993); see also Buxant & Saroglou (2008)

14 See several studies cited in Saroglou (2019, pp. 774–775); see, in addition, McPhetres et al. (2018)

15 Deak & Saroglou (2016), Shepperd et al. (2019)

16 Baumeister & Exline (1999), Saroglou (1992, 2002b)

17 Sasaki & Kim (2011), Stark (2001)

18 Laurin & Kay (2017) and McCullough & Carter (2013), for reviews; see also Kurt et al. (2018) and Minton et al. (2019)

19 Meier et al. (2007a, 2007b); see also Demoulin et al. (2008)

20 Galen & Miller (2011), Jackson & Esses (1997), Pichon & Saroglou (2009)

21 Johnson et al. (2011), Rade et al. (2017), Wright (2016)

22 Saroglou et al. (2009), Schumann et al. (2014), Tsang et al. (2020)

23 Cohen et al. (2006), Mullet & Azar (2009)

24 Lam & McCullough (2000), Stephenson et al. (2008)

25 Haggard et al. (2019), Schnabel (2016)

26 Batson et al. (1999), Blogowska & Saroglou (2011), Hoffarth et al. (2018)

27 Deak & Saroglou (2015, 2017)

28 Johnson et al. (2012)

29 Banyasz et al. (2016), de Regt (2012), Rowatt et al. (2014)

30 Arzheimer & Carter (2009), Lee et al. (2018)

31 Deslandes & Anderson (2019), Hansen & Ryder (2016), Shaver et al. (2016), Van Tongeren et al. (2016)

32 Clobert et al. (2015, 2017)

33 Batson et al. (1993), Blogowska & Saroglou (2013), Hall et al. (2010)

34 Jackson & Gray (2019)

35 Zuckerman et al. (2016); see also Sherkat & Lehman (2018)

36 Brandt & Van Tongeren (2017), Kossowska et al. (2017), Uzarevic & Saroglou (2020), Uzarevic et al. (2019)

37 For a review of research on religious morality in these domains, see Saroglou (2019)

CHAPTER 5

1 Oman & Syme (2018)

2 Wulff (2014), Yaden et al. (2017)

3 Meissner (1992), Saroglou (2006b)

4 Koenig et al. (2012), Loewenthal (2007)

5 Breslin & Lewis (2015), Galliford & Furnham (2017), Lindeman et al. (2015), Routledge et al. (2016), Willard & Norenzayan (2017)

6 Baker & Draper (2010), Francis & Williams (2009), Lindeman et al. (2015), Lindeman & Svedholm-Häkkinen (2016)

7 Lewis & Loewenthal (2018), Loewenthal (2007)

8 Examining specifically research on religion and OCD provides interesting insights that may be lost if one subordinates OCD under the broader category of anxiety disorders

9 Buchholz et al. (2019), Dèttore et al. (2017), Inozu et al. (2020), Sica et al. (2002), Siev et al. (2011), Williams et al. (2013)

10 Koenig et al. (2012)

11 Efrati (2019), Rigo & Saroglou (2018)

12 Efrati (2019), Grubbs et al. (2015), Kohut & Štulhofer (2018), Perry & Whitehead (2019), for sexual repression; Hackathorn et al. (2016), Higgins et al. (2010), for sexual satisfaction

13 Bell (1985), Huline-Dickens (2000)

14 Cohen et al. (2014)

15 Böhm et al. (2014), Calkins et al. (2015)

16 Gibbs & Goldbach (2015), McCann et al. (2020)

17 Diener et al. (2011), Gebauer et al. (2017b), Joshanloo & Weijers (2016a, 2016b), Lun & Bond (2013), Stavrova et al. (2013)

18 Bomhoff & Siah (2019)

19 Koenig et al. (2012), VanderWeele (2017), for reviews; Garssen et al. (2020), for a meta-analysis of 48 longitudinal studies

20 Koenig et al. (2012), VanderWeele (2017), for anxiety and depression; Jong et al. (2018), for death anxiety

21 Cheung & Yeung (2011), Koenig et al. (2012), Yeung et al. (2009)

22 Lawrence et al. (2016), Wu et al. (2015), for suicide; Ebert et al. (2020), Shor & Roelfs (2013), Wallace et al. (2019), for longevity

23 This is my synthesis of theory and research on the mediators of the religion-health relation; for other syntheses, see Koenig et al. (2012), Park & Slattery (2013)

24 Zuckerman et al. (2016), for a review; see also Baker et al. (2018), Yeniaras & Akarsu (2017)

25 Saroglou (2014a)

26 Exline (2013), Koenig et al. (2012)

27 Van Cappellen et al. (2013), Zukerman & Korn (2014)

28 Meuleman & Billiet (2011)

29 Granqvist (2020), Spilka & Ladd (2013)

30 Burris & Petrican (2014), Watts (2007)

31 Tsai et al. (2013), Van Cappellen & Rimé (2014)

32 Lim (2016), Ritter et al. (2014)

33 Mahoney (2010), Mahoney et al. (2001)

34 Mollidor et al. (2015), Yeung (2018)

35 Saroglou (2014a), Ysseldyk et al. (2010)

36 Gebauer et al. (2017a, 2018), Leszczensky et al. (2019)

37 Koenig et al. (2012), VanderWeele (2017)

38 Abu-Raiya & Pargament (2015), for a review

39 Saroglou & Anciaux (2004), Vishkin et al. (2016, 2019)

CHAPTER 6

1 Atran (2002), Boyer (2001), Kirkpatrick (2005)

2 Saroglou (2014a, 2015); see also Johnson (2012)

3 Freud (1927/1961)

REFERENCES

Aalsma, M. C., et al. (2013). Developmental trajectories of religiosity, sexual conservatism and sexual behavior among female adolescents. *Journal of Adolescence*, 36, 1193–1204.

Abu-Raiya, H., & Pargament, K. I. (2015). Religious coping among diverse religions: Commonalities and divergences. *Psychology of Religion and Spirituality*, 7, 24–33.

Arzheimer, K., & Carter, E. (2009). Christian religiosity and voting for West European radical right parties. *West European Politics*, 32, 985–1011.

Ashton, M. C. (2018). *Individual differences and personality* (3rd ed.). London, UK: Academic Press-Elsevier.

Ashton, M. C., & Lee, K. L. (2019). Religiousness and the HEXACO personality factors and facets in a large online sample. *Journal of Personality*, 87, 1103–1118.

Atran, S. (2002). *In gods we trust: The evolutionary landscape of religion*. New York, NY: Oxford University Press.

Baker, J. O., & Draper, S. (2010). Diverse supernatural portfolios: Certitude, exclusivity, and the curvilinear relationship between religiosity and paranormal beliefs. *Journal for the Scientific Study of Religion*, 49, 413–424.

Baker, J. O., Stroope, S., & Walker, M. H. (2018). Secularity, religiosity, and health: Physical and mental health differences between atheists, agnostics, and nonaffiliated theists compared to religiously affiliated individuals. *Social Science Research*, 75, 44–57.

Bamford, C., & Lagattuta, K. H. (2010). A new look at children's understanding of mind and emotion: The case of prayer. *Developmental Psychology*, 46, 78–92.

Banyasz, A. M., Tokar, D. M., & Kaut, K. P. (2016). Predicting religious ethnocentrism: Evidence for a partial mediation model. *Psychology of Religion and Spirituality*, 8, 25–34.

Barrett, J. L. (2012). *Born believers: The science of children's religious belief*. New York, NY: Free Press.

Batson, C. D., Floyd, R. B., Meyer, J. M., & Winner, A. L. (1999). "And who is my neighbor?": Intrinsic religion as a source of universal compassion. *Journal for the Scientific Study of Religion*, 38, 445–457.

Batson, C. D., Schoenrade, P., & Ventis, W. L. (1993). *Religion and the individual: A social psychological perspective*. New York, NY: Oxford University Press.

Baumeister, R. F., & Exline, J. J. (1999). Virtue, personality, and social relations: Self-control as the moral muscle. *Journal of Personality*, 67, 1165–1194.

Beit-Hallahmi, B. (2015). *Psychological perspectives on religion and religiosity*. Hove, UK: Routledge.

Bell, R. (1985). *Holy anorexia*. Chicago, IL: University of Chicago Press.

Blogowska, J., & Saroglou, V. (2011). Religious fundamentalism and limited prosociality as a function of the target. *Journal for the Scientific Study of Religion*, 50, 44–60.

Blogowska, J., & Saroglou, V. (2013). For better or worse: Fundamentalists' attitudes towards outgroups as a function of exposure to authoritative religious texts. *International Journal for the Psychology of Religion*, 23, 103–125.

Böhm, B., Zollner, H., Fegert, J. M., & Liebhardt, H. (2014). Child sexual abuse in the context of the Roman Catholic Church: A review of literature from 1981–2013. *Journal of Child Sexual Abuse*, 23, 635–656.

Bomhoff, E. J., & Siah, A. K. L. (2019). The relationship between income, religiosity and health: Their effects on life satisfaction. *Personality and Individual Differences*, 144, 168–173.

Boyer, P. (2001). *Religion explained: The evolutionary origins of religious thought*. New York, NY: Basic Books.

Brandt, M. J., & Van Tongeren, D. R. (2017). People both high and low on religious fundamentalism are prejudiced toward dissimilar groups. *Journal of Personality and Social Psychology*, 112, 76–97.

Breslin, M. J., & Lewis, C. A. (2015). Schizotypy and religiosity: The magic of prayer. *Archive for the Psychology of Religion*, 37, 84–97.

Buchholz, J. L., et al. (2019). Scrupulosity, religious affiliation and symptom presentation in obsessive compulsive disorder. *Behavioural and Cognitive Psychotherapy*, 47, 478–492.

Burris, C. T., & Petrican, R. (2014). Religion, negative emotions, and regulation. In V. Saroglou (Ed.), *Religion, personality, and social behavior* (pp. 96–122). New York, NY: Psychology Press.

Busch, J. T. A., Watson-Jones, R. E., & Legare, C. H. (2017). The coexistence of natural and supernatural explanations within and across domains and development. *British Journal of Developmental Psychology*, 35, 4–20.

Buxant, C., & Saroglou, V. (2008). Feeling good, but lacking autonomy: Closed-mindedness on social and moral issues in new religious movements. *Journal of Religion and Health*, 47, 17–31.

Calkins, C., Fargo, J., Jeglic, E., & Terry, K. (2015). Blessed be the children: A case-control study of sexual abusers in the Catholic Church. *Behavioral Sciences and the Law*, 33, 580–594.

Cheung, C.-K., & Yeung, J. W.-K. (2011). Meta-analysis of relationships between religiosity and constructive and destructive behaviors among adolescents. *Children and Youth Services Review*, 33, 376–385.

Clobert, M., & Saroglou, V. (2015). Religion, paranormal beliefs, and distrust in science: Comparing East versus West. *Archive for the Psychology of Religion*, 37, 185–199.

Clobert, M., Saroglou, V., & Hwang, K.-K. (2015). Buddhist concepts as implicitly reducing prejudice and increasing prosociality. *Personality and Social Psychology Bulletin*, 41, 513–525.

Clobert, M., Saroglou, V., & Hwang, K.-K. (2017). East Asian religious tolerance vs. Western monotheist prejudice: The role of (in)tolerance of contradiction. *Group Processes and Intergroup Relations*, 20, 216–232.

Cohen, A. B., Gorvine, B. J., & Gorvine, H. (2013). The religion, spirituality, and psychology of Jews. In K. I. Pargament, J. J. Exline, & J. W. Jones (Eds.), *APA handbook of psychology, religion, and spirituality* (Vol. 1, pp. 665–679). Washington, DC: American Psychological Association.

Cohen, A. B., Malka, A., Rozin, P., & Cherfas, L. (2006). Religion and unforgivable offenses. *Journal of Personality*, 74, 85–118.

Cohen, D., Kim, E., & Hudson, N. W. (2014). Religion, the forbidden, and sublimation. *Current Directions in Psychological Science*, 23, 208–214.

Colzato, L. S., et al. (2010). God: Do I have your attention? *Cognition*, 117, 87–94.

Copen, C. E., & Silverstein, M. (2008). The transmission of religious beliefs across generations: Do grandparents matter? *Journal of Comparative Family Studies, 39,* 59–71.

Cribari-Neto, F., & Souza, T. C. (2013). Religious belief and intelligence: Worldwide evidence. *Intelligence, 41,* 482–489.

Deak, C., & Saroglou, V. (2015). Opposing abortion, gay adoption, euthanasia, and suicide: Compassionate openness or self-centered moral rigorism? *Archive for the Psychology of Religion, 37,* 267–294.

Deak, C., & Saroglou, V. (2016). Valuing care protects religiosity from the antisocial consequences of impersonal deontology. *Journal of Empirical Theology, 29,* 171–189.

Deak, C., & Saroglou, V. (2017). Terminating a child's life? Religious, moral, cognitive, and emotional factors underlying non-acceptance of child euthanasia. *Psychologica Belgica, 57,* 59–67.

Demoulin, S., Saroglou, V., & Van Pachterbeke, M. (2008). Infra-humanizing others, supra-humanizing gods: The emotional hierarchy. *Social Cognition, 26,* 235–247.

de Regt, S. (2012). Religiosity as a moderator of the relationship between authoritarianism and social dominance orientation: A cross-cultural comparison. *International Journal for the Psychology of Religion, 22,* 31–41.

Deslandes, C., & Anderson, J. R. (2019). Religion and prejudice toward immigrants and refugees: A meta-analytic review. *International Journal for the Psychology of Religion, 29,* 128–145.

Dèttore, D., Berardi, D., & Pozza, A. (2017). Religious affiliation and obsessive cognitions and symptoms: A comparison between Jews, Christians, and Muslims in non-clinical groups in Italy. *Psychology of Religion and Spirituality, 9,* 348–357.

Diener, E., Tay, L., & Myers, D. G. (2011). The religion paradox: If religion makes people happy, why are so many dropping out? *Journal of Personality and Social Psychology, 101,* 1278–1290.

Dunham, Y., Srinivasan, M., Dotsch, R., & Barner, D. (2014). Religion insulates ingroup evaluations: The development of intergroup attitudes in India. *Developmental Science, 17,* 311–319.

Duriez, B., Dezutter, J., Neyrinck, B., & Hutsebaut, D. (2007). An introduction to the post-critical belief scale: Internal structure and external relationships. *Psyke and Logos, 28,* 767–793.

Ebert, T., Gebauer, J. E., Talman, J. R., & Rentfrow, P. J. (2020). Religious people only live longer in religious cultural contexts: A gravestone analysis. *Journal of Personality and Social Psychology, 119,* 1–6.

Efrati, Y. (2019). God, I can't stop thinking about sex! The rebound effect in unsuccessful suppression of sexual thoughts among religious adolescents. *Journal of Sex Research, 56,* 146–155.

Erlandsson, A., Nilsson, A., Tinghög, G., & Västfjäll, D. (2018). Bullshit-sensitivity predicts prosocial behavior. *PLoS One, 13*(7), e0201474.

Evans, E. M., & Lane, J. D. (2011). Contradictory or complementary? Creationist and evolutionist explanations of the origin(s) of species. *Human Development, 54,* 144–159.

Exline, J. J. (2013). Religious and spiritual struggles. In K. I. Pargament, J. J. Exline, & J. W. Jones (Eds.), *APA handbook of psychology, religion, and spirituality* (Vol. 1, pp. 459–475). Washington, DC: American Psychological Association.

Fowler, J. W. (1981). *Stages of faith: The psychology of human development and the quest for meaning.* San Francisco, CA: Harper & Row.

Francis, L. J., & Penny, G. (2014). Gender differences in religion. In V. Saroglou (Ed.), *Religion, personality, and social behavior* (pp. 313–337). New York, NY: Psychology Press.

Francis, L. J., & Williams, E. (2009). Alternative spiritualities: Different personalities? An enquiry concerning paranormal beliefs and traditional religiosity. *Research in the Social Scientific Study of Religion, 20,* 69–84.

Freud, S. (1961). *The future of an illusion* (J. Strachey, Trans.). New York: Norton. (Original work published 1927).

Galen, L. W. (2012). Does religious belief promote prosociality? A critical examination. *Psychological Bulletin, 138,* 876–906.

Galen, L. W., & Miller, T. R. (2011). Perceived deservingness of outcomes as a function of religious fundamentalism and target responsibility. *Journal of Applied Social Psychology, 41,* 2144–2164.

Galliford, N., & Furnham, A. (2017). Individual difference factors and beliefs in medical and political conspiracy theories. *Scandinavian Journal of Psychology, 58,* 422–428.

Garssen, B., Visser, A., & Pool, G. (2020). Does spirituality or religion positively affect mental health? Meta-analysis of longitudinal studies. *International Journal for the Psychology of Religion.* Advance online publication.

Gebauer, J. E., Bleidorn, W., Gosling, S. D., Rentfrow, P. J., Lamb, M. E., & Potter, J. (2014). Cross-cultural variations in Big Five relationships with religiosity: A sociocultural motives perspective. *Journal of Personality and Social Psychology*, 107, 1064–1091.

Gebauer, J. E., Sedikides, C., & Schrade, A. (2017a). Christian self-enhancement. *Journal of Personality and Social Psychology*, 113, 786–809.

Gebauer, J. E., et al. (2017b). The religiosity as social value hypothesis: A multi-method replication and extension across 65 countries and three levels of spatial aggregation. *Journal of Personality and Social Psychology*, 113, e18–e39.

Gebauer, J. E. et al. (2018). Mind-body practices and the self: Yoga and meditation do not quiet the ego, but instead boost self-enhancement. *Psychological Science*, 29, 1299–1308.

Gibbs, J. J., & Goldbach, J. (2015). Religious conflict, sexual identity, and suicidal behaviors among LGBT young adults. *Archives of Suicide Research*, 19, 472–488.

Glick, L. B. (2013). Defying the Enlightenment: Jewish ethnicity and ethnic circumcision. In G. C. Denniston, F. M. Hodges, & M. F. Milos (Eds.), *Genital cutting: Protecting children from medical, cultural, and religious infringements* (pp. 284–296). New York, NY: Springer.

Goldstein, T. R., & Woolley, J. D. (2016). Ho! Ho! who? Parent promotion of belief and live encounters with Santa Claus. *Cognitive Development*, 39, 113–129.

Good, M., & Willoughby, T. (2008). Adolescence as a sensitive period for spiritual development. *Child Development Perspectives*, 2, 32–37.

Granqvist, P. (2020). *Attachment in religion and spirituality: A wider view*. New York, NY: Guilford.

Grubbs, J. B., Exline, J. J., Pargament, K. I., Hook, J. N., & Carlisle, R. D. (2015). Transgression as addiction: Religiosity and moral disapproval as predictors of perceived addiction to pornography. *Archives of Sexual Behavior*, 44, 125–136.

Grubbs, J. B., Exline, J. J., Pargament, K. I., Volk, F., & Lindberg, M. J. (2017). Internet pornography use, perceived addiction, and religious/spiritual struggles. *Archives of Sexual Behavior*, 46, 1733–1745.

Hackathorn, J. M., Ashdown, B. K., & Rife, S. C. (2016). The sacred bed: Sex guilt mediates religiosity and satisfaction for unmarried people. *Sexuality and Culture: An Interdisciplinary Quarterly*, 20, 153–172.

Haggard, M. C., Kaelen, R., Saroglou, V., Klein, O., & Rowatt, W. C. (2019). Religion's role in the illusion of gender equality: Supraliminal and subliminal religious priming increases benevolent sexism. *Psychology of Religion and Spirituality*, 11, 392–398.

Hall, D., Matz, D. C., & Wood, W. (2010). Why don't we practice what we preach? A meta-analytic review of religious racism. *Personality and Social Psychology Review*, 14, 126–139.

Hansen, I. G., & Ryder, A. (2016). In search of "religion proper": Intrinsic religiosity and coalitional rigidity make opposing predictions of intergroup hostility across religious groups. *Journal of Cross-Cultural Psychology*, 47, 835–857.

Hardman, C. E. (2004). Children in new religious movements. In J. R. Lewis (Ed.), *The Oxford handbook of new religious movements* (pp. 386–416). Oxford, UK: Oxford University Press.

Hardy, S. A., White, J. A., Zhang, Z., & Ruchty, J. (2011). Parenting and the socialization of religiousness and spirituality. *Psychology of Religion and Spirituality*, 3, 217–230.

Harper, C. A., & Perkins, C. (2018). Reporting child sexual abuse within religious settings: Challenges and future directions. *Child Abuse Review*, 27, 30–41.

Harris, P. L., Koenig, M. A., Corriveau, K. H., & Jaswal, V. K. (2018). Cognitive foundations of learning from testimony. *Annual Review of Psychology*, 69, 251–273.

Heiden-Rootes, K., Wiegand, A., & Bono, D. (2019). Sexual minority adults: A national survey on depression, religious fundamentalism, parent relationship quality and acceptance. *Journal of Marital and Family Therapy*, 45, 106–119.

Heiphetz, L., Lane, J. D., Waytz, A., & Young, L. L. (2016). How children and adults represent God's mind. *Cognitive Science*, 40, 121–144.

Heiphetz, L., Lane, J. D., Waytz, A., & Young, L. L. (2018). My mind, your mind, and God's mind: How children and adults conceive of different agents' moral beliefs. *British Journal of Developmental Psychology*, 36, 467–481.

Heiphetz, L., Spelke, E. S., & Banaji, M. R. (2013). Patterns of implicit and explicit attitudes in children and adults: Tests in the domain of religion. *Journal of Experimental Psychology: General*, 142, 864–879.

Hermann, A., & Fuller, R. (2017). Trait narcissism and contemporary religious trends? *Archive for the Psychology of Religion*, 39, 99–117.

Higgins, J. A., Trussell, J., Moore, N. B., & Davidson, J. K. (2010). Virginity lost, satisfaction gained? Physiological and psychological sexual satisfaction at heterosexual debut. *Journal of Sex Research*, 47, 384–394.

Hoffarth, M. R., Hodson, G., & Molnar, D. S. (2018). When and why is religious attendance associated with antigay bias and gay rights opposition? A justification-suppression model approach. *Journal of Personality and Social Psychology*, 115, 526–563.

Hood, R. W., Jr., & Belzen, J. A. (2013). Research methods in the psychology of religion and spirituality. In R. F. Paloutzian & C. L. Park (Eds.), *Handbook of the psychology of religion and spirituality* (2nd ed., pp. 75–93). New York, NY: Guilford.

Hui, C. H., Cheung, S.-H., Lam, J., Lau, E. Y. Y., Cheung, S.-F., & Yuliawati, L. (2018). Psychological changes during faith exit: A three-year prospective study. *Psychology of Religion and Spirituality*, 10, 103–118.

Huline-Dickens, S. (2000). Anorexia nervosa: Some connections with the religious attitude. *British Journal of Medical Psychology*, 73, 67–76.

Inozu, M., Kahya, Y., & Yorulmaz, O. (2020). Neuroticism and religiosity: The role of obsessive beliefs, thought-control strategies and guilt in scrupulosity and obsessive – compulsive symptoms among Muslim undergraduates. *Journal of Religion and Health*, 59, 1140–1160.

Jackson, J. C., & Gray, K. (2019). When a good god makes bad people: Testing a theory of religion and immorality. *Journal of Personality and Social Psychology*, 117, 1203–1230.

Jackson, L. M., & Esses, V. M. (1997). Of scripture and ascription: The relation between religious fundamentalism and intergroup helping. *Personality and Social Psychology Bulletin*, 23, 893–906.

James, W. (1985). *The varieties of religious experience: A study in human nature*. Cambridge, MA: Harvard University Press. (Original work published 1902)

Johnson, D. (2012). What are atheists for? Hypotheses on the functions of non-belief in the evolution of religion. *Religion, Brain and Behavior*, 2, 48–70.

Johnson, M. K., Rowatt, W. C., Barnard-Brak, L. M., Patock-Peckham, J. A., LaBouff, J. P., & Carlisle, R. D. (2011). A mediational analysis of the role of right-wing authoritarianism and religious fundamentalism in the religiosity–prejudice link. *Personality and Individual Differences*, 50, 851–856.

Johnson, M. K., Rowatt, W. C., & LaBouff, J. P. (2012). Religiosity and prejudice revisited: In-group favoritism, out-group derogation, or both? *Psychology of Religion and Spirituality*, 4, 154–168.

Jong, J. (2013). Implicit measures in the experimental psychology of religion. In G. Dawes & J. Maclaurin (Eds.), *A new science of religion* (pp. 65–78). New York, NY: Routledge.

Jong, J., & Halberstadt, J. (2018). *Death anxiety and religious belief: An existential psychology of religion*. London, UK: Bloomsbury.

Jong, J., Ross, R., Philip, T., Chang, S.-H., Simons, N., & Halberstadt, J. (2018). The religious correlates of death anxiety: A systematic review and meta-analysis. *Religion, Brain and Behavior*, 8, 4–20.

Joshanloo, M., & Weijers, D. (2016a). Religiosity moderates the relationship between income inequality and life satisfaction across the globe. *Social Indicators Research*, 128, 731–750.

Joshanloo, M., & Weijers, D. (2016b). Religiosity reduces the negative influence of injustice on subjective well-being: A study in 121 nations. *Applied Research in Quality of Life*, 11, 601–612.

Kelley, J., & De Graaf, N. D. (1997). National context, parental socialization, and religious belief: Results from 15 nations. *American Sociological Review*, 62, 639–659.

King, P. E., & Boyatzis, C. J. (2015). Religious and spiritual development. In M. E. Lamb & R. M. Lerner (Eds.), *Handbook of child psychology and developmental science* (Vol. 3, 7th ed., pp. 975–1021). Hoboken, NJ: Wiley.

Kirkpatrick, L. A. (2005). *Attachment, evolution, and the psychology of religion*. New York, NY: Guilford.

Koenig, H., King, D., & Carson, V. B. (2012). *Handbook of religion and health* (2nd ed.). New York, NY: Oxford University Press.

Kohut, T., & Štulhofer, A. (2018). The role of religiosity in adolescents' compulsive pornography use: A longitudinal assessment. *Journal of Sex and Marital Therapy*, 44, 759–775.

Kossowska, M., Czernatowicz-Kukuczka, A., & Sekerdej, M. (2017). Many faces of dogmatism: Prejudice as a way of protecting certainty against value violators among dogmatic believers and atheists. *British Journal of Psychology*, 108, 127–147.

Krause, N. (2013). Religious involvement in the later years of life. In K. I. Pargament, J. J. Exline, & J. W. Jones (Eds.), *APA handbook of psychology, religion, and spirituality* (Vol. 1, pp. 529–545). Washington, DC: American Psychological Association.

Kurt, D., Inman, J. J., & Gino, F. (2018). Religious shoppers spend less money. *Journal of Experimental Social Psychology*, 78, 116–124.

Lam, W. A., & McCullough, L. B. (2000). Influence of religious and spiritual values on the willingness of Chinese Americans to donate organs for transplantation. *Clinical Transplantation*, 14, 449–456.

Lane, J. D., Evans, E. M., Brink, K. A., & Wellman, H. M. (2016). Developing concepts of ordinary and extraordinary communication. *Developmental Psychology*, 52, 19–30.

Lane, J. D., & Harris, P. L. (2014). Confronting, representing, and believing counterintuitive concepts: Navigating the natural and the supernatural. *Perspectives on Psychological Science*, 9, 144–160.

Laurin, K., & Kay, A. C. (2017). The motivational underpinnings of belief in God. In J. M. Olson (Ed.), *Advances in experimental social psychology* (Vol. 56, pp. 201–257). London, UK: Academic Press.

Lawrence, R. E., Oquendo, M. A., & Stanley, B. (2016). Religion and suicide risk: A systematic review. *Archives of Suicide Research*, 20, 1–21.

Leach, M. M., Piedmont, R. L., & Monteiro, D. (2001). Images of god among Christians, Hindus, and Muslims in India. *Research in the Social Scientific Study of Religion*, 12, 207–225.

Lee, B. H. J., Pearce, L. D., & Schorpp, K. M. (2017). Religious pathways from adolescence to adulthood. *Journal for the Scientific Study of Religion*, 56, 678–689.

Lee, K., Ashton, M. C., Griep, Y., & Edmonds, M. (2018). Personality, religion, and politics: An investigation in 33 countries. *European Journal of Personality*, 32, 100–115.

Legare, C. H., Evans, E. M., Rosengren, K. S., & Harris, P. L. (2012). The coexistence of natural and supernatural explanations across cultures and development. *Child Development*, 83, 779–793.

Leszczensky, L., Flache, A., & Sauter, L. (2019). Does the share of religious ingroup members affect how important religion is to adolescents? Applying optimal distinctiveness theory to four European countries. *Journal of Ethnic and Migration Studies*. Advance online publication.

Lewis, C. A., & Loewenthal, K. M. (Eds.). (2018). Religion and obsessionality: Obsessive actions and religious practices [special issue]. *Mental Health, Religion and Culture*, 21(2).

Lim, C. (2016). Religion, time use, and affective well-being. *Sociological Science*, 3, 685–709.

Lindeman, M., & Svedholm-Häkkinen, A. M. (2016). Does poor understanding of physical world predict religious and paranormal beliefs? *Applied Cognitive Psychology*, 30, 736–742.

Lindeman, M., Svedholm-Häkkinen, A. M., & Lipsanen, J. (2015). Ontological confusions but not mentalizing abilities predict religious belief, paranormal belief, and belief in supernatural purpose. *Cognition*, 134, 63–76.

Loewenthal, K. M. (2007). *Religion, culture and mental health*. Cambridge, UK: Cambridge University Press.

Lun, V. M.-C., & Bond, M. H. (2013). Examining the relation of religion and spirituality to subjective well-being across national cultures. *Psychology of Religion and Spirituality, 5*, 304–315.

Mahoney, A. (2010). Religion in families, 1999–2009: A relational spirituality framework. *Journal of Marriage and Family, 72*, 805–827.

Mahoney, A., Pargament, K. I., Tarakeshwar, N., & Swank, A. B. (2001). Religion in the home in the 1980s and 1990s: A meta-analytic review and conceptual analysis of links between religion, marriage, and parenting. *Journal of Family Psychology, 15*, 559–596.

McCann, E., Donohue, G., & Timmins, F. (2020). An exploration of the relationship between spirituality, religion and mental health among youth who identify as LGBT: A systematic literature review. *Journal of Religion and Health, 59*, 828–844.

McCullough, M. E., & Carter, E. C. (2013). Religion, self-control, and self-regulation: How and why are they related? In K. I. Pargament, J. J. Exline, & J. W. James (Eds.), *APA handbook of psychology, religion, and spirituality* (Vol. 1, pp. 123–138). Washington, DC: American Psychological Association.

McNamara Barry, C., & Abo-Zena, M. M. (Eds.). (2014). *Emerging adults' religiousness and spirituality*. New York, NY: Oxford University Press.

McPhetres, J., Conway, P., Hughes, J. S., & Zuckerman, M. (2018). Reflecting on God's will: Reflective processing contributes to religious peoples' deontological dilemma responses. *Journal of Experimental Social Psychology, 79*, 301–314.

Meier, B. P., Hauser, D. J., Robinson, M. D., Kelland Friesen, C., & Schjeldahl, K. (2007a). What's "up" with God? Vertical space as a representation of the divine. *Journal of Personality and Social Psychology, 93*, 699–710.

Meier, B. P., Sellbom, M., & Wygant, D. B. (2007b). Failing to take the moral high ground: Psychopathy and the vertical representation of morality. *Personality and Individual Differences, 43*, 757–767.

Meissner, W. W. (1992). *Ignatius of Loyola: The psychology of a saint*. New Haven, CT: Yale University Press.

Meuleman, B., & Billiet, J. (2011). Religious involvement: Its relation to values and social attitudes. In E. Davidov, P. Schmidt, & J. Billiet (Eds.), *Cross-cultural analysis: Methods and applications* (pp. 173–206). New York, NY: Routledge.

Minton, E. A., Johnson, K. A., & Liu, R. L. (2019). Religiosity and special food consumption: The explanatory effects of moral priorities. *Journal of Business Research*, *95*, 442–454.

Mollidor, C., Hancock, N., & Pepper, M. (2015). Volunteering, religiosity and well-being: Interrelationships among Australian churchgoers. *Mental Health, Religion and Culture*, *18*, 20–32.

Müller, T. S., De Graaf, N. D., & Schmidt, P. (2014). Which societies provide a strong religious socialization context? Explanations beyond the effects of national religiosity. *Journal for the Scientific Study of Religion*, *53*, 739–759.

Mullet, E., & Azar, F. (2009). Apologies, repentance, and forgiveness: A Muslim-Christian comparison. *International Journal for the Psychology of Religion*, *19*, 275–285.

Nelsen, H. M. (1990). The religious identification of children of interfaith marriages. *Review of Religious Research*, *32*, 122–134.

Nilsson, S. (2016). Children in new religions. In J. R. Lewis & I. B. Tøllefsen (Eds.), *The Oxford handbook of new religious movements* (Vol. 2, pp. 248–263). Oxford, UK: Oxford University Press.

Norenzayan, A. (2016). Theodiversity. *Annual Review of Psychology*, *67*, 21.1–21.24.

Norenzayan, A., Atran, S., Faulkner, J., & Schaller, M. (2006). Memory and mystery: The cultural selection of minimally counterintuitive narratives. *Cognitive Science*, *30*, 531–553.

Nucci, L., & Turiel, E. (1993). God's word, religious rules, and their relation to Christian and Jewish children's concepts of morality. *Child Development*, *64*, 1475–1491.

Nyhof, M. A., & Johnson, C. N. (2017). Is God just a big person? Children's conceptions of god across cultures and religious traditions. *British Journal of Developmental Psychology*, *35*, 60–75.

Oman, D., & Syme, S. L. (2018). Weighing the evidence: What is revealed by 100+ meta analyses and systematic reviews of religion/spirituality and health? In D. Oman (Ed.), *Why religion and spirituality matter for public health* (pp. 261–281). Cham, Switzerland: Springer.

Oser, F. K., Scarlett, W. G., & Bucher, A. (2006). Religious and spiritual development throughout the life span. In W. Damon & R. L. Lerner (Eds.), *Handbook of child psychology* (Vol. 1, 6th ed., pp. 942–998). Hoboken, NJ: Wiley.

Park, C. L., & Slattery, J. M. (2013). Religion, spirituality, and mental health. In R. F. Paloutzian & C. L. Park (Eds.), *Handbook of the psychology of religion and spirituality* (2nd ed., pp. 540–559). New York, NY: Guilford.

Pennycook, G., Cheyne, J. A., Barr, N., Koehler, D. J., & Fugelsang, J. A. (2015). On the reception and detection of pseudo-profound bullshit. *Judgment and Decision Making*, 10, 549–563.

Pennycook, G., Ross, R. M., Koehler, D. J., & Fugelsang, J. A. (2016). Atheists and agnostics are more reflective than religious believers: Four empirical studies and a meta-analysis. *PLoS One*, 11(4), e0153039.

Perry, S. L., & Whitehead, A. L. (2019). Only bad for believers? Religion, pornography use, and sexual satisfaction among American men. *Journal of Sex Research*, 56, 50–61.

Pew Research Center. (2015). *The future of world religions: Population growth projections, 2010–2050.* Retrieved from www.pewforum.org/

Pew Research Center. (2016). *The gender gap in religion around the world.* Retrieved from www.pewforum.org/

Pew Research Center. (2017). *The changing global religious landscape.* Retrieved from www.pewforum.org/

Pew Research Center. (2018a). *Eastern and Western Europeans differ on importance of religion, views of minorities, and key social issues.* Retrieved from www.pewforum.org/

Pew Research Center. (2018b). *The age gap in religion around the world.* Retrieved from www.pewforum.org/

Phalet, K., Fleischmann, F., & Hillekens, J. (2018). Religious identity and acculturation of immigrant minority youth: Toward a contextual and developmental approach. *European Psychologist*, 23, 32–43.

Pichon, I., Boccato, G., & Saroglou, V. (2007). Nonconscious influences of religion on prosociality: A priming study. *European Journal of Social Psychology*, 37, 1032–1045.

Pichon, I., & Saroglou, V. (2009). Religion and helping: Impact of target, thinking styles and just-world beliefs. *Archive for the Psychology of Religion*, 31, 215–236.

Piedmont, R. L. (1999). Does spirituality represent the sixth factor of personality? Spiritual transcendence and the five-factor model. *Journal of Personality*, 67, 983–1013.

Rade, C. B., Holland, A. M., Gregory, J. B., & Desmarais, S. L. (2017). Systematic review of religious affiliations and beliefs as correlates of public attitudes toward capital punishment. *Criminal Justice Studies: A Critical Journal of Crime, Law & Society*, 30, 63–85.

Rigo, C., & Saroglou, V. (2018). Religiosity and sexual behavior: Tense relationships and underlying affects and cognitions in samples of Christian and Muslim tradition. *Archive for the Psychology of Religion*, 40, 176–201.

Ritter, R. S., Preston, J. L., & Hernandez, I. (2014). Happy tweets: Christians are happier, more socially connected, and less analytical than atheists on twitter. *Social Psychological and Personality Science, 5,* 243–249.

Roccas, S., & Elster, A. (2014). Values and religiosity. In V. Saroglou (Ed.), *Religion, personality, and social behavior* (pp. 193–212). New York, NY: Psychology Press.

Rosengren, K. S., Johnson, C. N., & Harris, P. L. (Eds.). (2000). *Imagining the impossible: Magical, scientific, and religious thinking in children.* New York, NY: Cambridge University Press.

Routledge, C., Abeyta, A. A., & Roylance, C. (2016). An existential function of evil: The effects of religiosity and compromised meaning on belief in magical evil forces. *Motivation and Emotion, 40,* 681–688.

Rowatt, W. C., Carpenter, T., & Haggard, M. (2014). Religion, prejudice, and intergroup relations. In V. Saroglou (Ed.), *Religion, personality, and social behavior* (pp. 170–192). New York, NY: Psychology Press.

Rowatt, W. C., Shen, M. J., LaBouff, J. P., & Gonzalez, A. (2013). Religious fundamentalism, right-wing authoritarianism, and prejudice. In R. F. Paloutzian & C. L. Park (Eds.), *Handbook of psychology of religion and spirituality* (2nd ed., pp. 457–475). New York, NY: Guilford.

Różycka-Tran, J. (2017). Love thy neighbor? The effects of religious in/out-group identity on social behavior. *Personality and Individual Differences, 115,* 7–12.

Rubin, O. D., & Rubin, A. (2014). Intergenerational religious transmission mechanisms among second-generation migrants: The case of Jewish immigrants in the United States. *International Journal of Intercultural Relations, 43,* 265–277.

Sabato, H., & Kogut, T. (2018). The association between religiousness and children's altruism: The role of the recipient's neediness. *Developmental Psychology, 54,* 1363–1371.

Saroglou, V. (1992). *Rêve et spiritualité chez Jean Climaque [Dreams and spirituality in John Climacus].* Unpublished master's thesis in religious sciences, Université catholique de Louvain.

Saroglou, V. (2002a). Beyond dogmatism: The need for closure as related to religion. *Mental Health, Religion, and Culture, 5,* 183–194.

Saroglou, V. (2002b). Religion and sense of humor: An a priori incompatibility? Theoretical considerations from a psychological perspective. *Humor: International Journal of Humor Research, 15,* 191–214.

Saroglou, V. (2006a). "A son image" mais "à Sa ressemblance" ou comment l'homme façonne Dieu: Dynamiques psychologiques. In O. H. Pesch &

J.- M. Van Cangh (Eds.), *L'homme, image de Dieu* (pp. 145–187). Bruxelles, Belgium: Cerf.

Saroglou, V. (2006b). Saints et héros: Vies parallèles et psychologies spécifiques. *Revue Théologique de Louvain, 37*, 313–341.

Saroglou, V. (2010). Religiousness as a cultural adaptation of basic traits: A five factor model perspective. *Personality and Social Psychology Review, 14*, 108–125.

Saroglou, V. (2011). Believing, bonding, behaving, and belonging: The big four religious dimensions and cultural variation. *Journal of Cross-Cultural Psychology, 42*, 1320–1340.

Saroglou, V. (2012). Adolescents' social development and the role of religion: Coherence at the detriment of openness. In G. Trommsdorff & X. Chen (Eds.), *Values, religion, and culture in adolescent development* (pp. 391–423). Cambridge, UK: Cambridge University Press.

Saroglou, V. (2013). Religion, spirituality, and altruism. In K. I. Pargament, J. J. Exline, & J. W. Jones (Eds.), *APA handbook of psychology, religion and spirituality* (Vol. 1, pp. 439–457). Washington, DC: American Psychological Association.

Saroglou, V. (2014a). Conclusion: Understanding religion and irreligion. In V. Saroglou (Ed.), *Religion, personality, and social behavior* (pp. 361–391). New York, NY: Psychology Press.

Saroglou, V. (2014b). Introduction: Studying religion in personality and social psychology. In V. Saroglou (Ed.), *Religion, personality, and social behavior* (pp. 1–28). New York, NY: Psychology Press.

Saroglou, V. (2015, March). *Believers and atheists: An evolutionary understanding of individual differences in religiosity, their stability and change.* Invited talk at the integrative symposium "Religion past and present: Origins and functions of spirituality." Inaugural International Convention of Psychological Science, Amsterdam, the Netherlands.

Saroglou, V. (2016). Intergroup conflict, religious fundamentalism, and culture. *Journal of Cross-Cultural Psychology, 47*, 33–41.

Saroglou, V. (2017). Culture, personality, and religiosity. In A. T. Church (Ed.), *The Praeger handbook of personality across cultures* (Vol. 2, pp. 153–184). Santa Barbara, CA: Praeger.

Saroglou, V. (2019). Religion and related morality across cultures. In D. Matsumoto & H. C. Hwang (Eds.), *Handbook of culture and psychology* (2nd ed.). New York, NY: Oxford University Press.

Saroglou, V., & Anciaux, L. (2004). Liking sick humor: Coping styles and religion as predictors. *Humor: International Journal of Humor Research*, 17, 257–277.

Saroglou, V., Buxant, C., & Tilquin, J. (2008). Positive emotions as leading to religion and spirituality. *Journal of Positive Psychology*, 3, 165–173.

Saroglou, V., & Cohen, A. B. (2013). Cultural and cross-cultural psychology of religion. In R. F. Paloutzian & C. L. Park (Eds.), *Handbook of the psychology of religion and spirituality* (2nd ed., pp. 330–353). New York: Guilford.

Saroglou, V., Corneille, O., & Van Cappellen, P. (2009). "Speak, Lord, your servant is listening": Religious priming activates submissive thoughts and behaviors. *International Journal for the Psychology of Religion*, 19, 143–154.

Saroglou, V., Karim, M., & Day, J. M. (in press). Personality and values of deconverts: A function of current nonbelief or prior religious socialization? *Mental Health, Religion, and Culture*.

Saroglou, V., & Muñoz-García, A. (2008). Individual differences in religion and spirituality: An issue of personality traits and/or values. *Journal for the Scientific Study of Religion*, 47, 83–101.

Saroglou, V., Pichon, I. Trompette, L., Verschueren, M., & Dernelle, R. (2005). Prosocial behavior and religion: New evidence based on projective measures and peer ratings. *Journal for the Scientific Study of Religion*, 44, 323–348.

Sasaki, J. Y., & Kim, H. S. (2011). At the intersection of culture and religion: A cultural analysis of religion's implications for secondary control and social affiliation. *Journal of Personality and Social Psychology*, 101, 401–414.

Saucier, G., et al. (2015). Cross-cultural differences in a global "Survey of World Views." *Journal of Cross-Cultural Psychology*, 46, 53–70.

Saucier, G., & Skrzypińska, K. (2006). Spiritual but not religious? Evidence for two independent dispositions. *Journal of Personality*, 74, 1257–1292.

Schnabel, L. (2016). Religion and gender equality worldwide: A country-level analysis. *Social Indicators Research*, 129, 893–907.

Schumann, K., McGregor, I., Nash, K. A., & Ross, M. (2014). Religious magnanimity: Reminding people of their religious belief system reduces hostility after threat. *Journal of Personality and Social Psychology*, 107, 432–453.

Schwadel, P. (2016). Does higher education cause religious decline? A longitudinal analysis of the within- and between-person effects of higher education on religiosity. *The Sociological Quarterly*, 57, 759–786.

Sedikides, C., & Gebauer, J. E. (2014). Religion and the self. In V. Saroglou (Ed.), *Religion, personality, and social behavior* (pp. 46–70). New York, NY: Psychology Press.

Shariff, A. F., & Norenzayan, A. (2007). God is watching you: Priming God concepts increases prosocial behavior in an anonymous economic game. *Psychological Science, 18*, 803–809.

Shariff, A. F., Willard, A. K., Andersen, T., & Norenzayan, A. (2016). Religious priming: A meta-analysis with a focus on prosociality. *Personality and Social Psychology Review, 20*, 27–48.

Shaver, J. H., Troughton, G., Sibley, C. G., & Bulbulia, J. A. (2016). Religion and the unmaking of prejudice toward Muslims: Evidence from a large national sample. *PLoS One, 11*, Article e0150209.

Shepperd, J. A., Pogge, G., Lipsey, N. P., Smith, C. T., & Miller, W. A. (2019). The link between religiousness and prejudice: Testing competing explanations in an adolescent sample. *Psychology of Religion and Spirituality*. Advance online publication.

Sherkat, D. E., & Lehman, D. (2018). Bad Samaritans: Religion and anti-immigrant and anti-Muslim sentiment in the United States. *Social Science Quarterly, 99*, 1791–1804.

Shor, E., & Roelfs, D. J. (2013). The longevity effects of religious and nonreligious participation: A meta-analysis and meta-regression. *Journal for the Scientific Study of Religion, 52*, 120–145.

Sica, C., Novara, C., & Sanavio, E. (2002). Religiousness and obsessive-compulsive cognitions and symptoms in an Italian population. *Behaviour Research and Therapy, 40*, 813–823.

Siev, J., Steketee, G., Fama, J. M., & Wilhelm, S. (2011). Cognitive and clinical characteristics of sexual and religious obsessions. *Journal of Cognitive Psychotherapy, 25*, 167–176.

Spilka, B., & Ladd, K. L. (2013). *The psychology of prayer: A scientific approach.* New York, NY: Guilford.

Stark, R. (2001). Gods, rituals, and the moral order. *Journal for the Scientific Study of Religion, 40*, 619–636.

Stavrova, O., Fetchenhauer, D., & Schlösser, T. (2013). Why are religious people happy? The effect of the social norm of religiosity across countries. *Social Science Research, 42*, 90–105.

Stephenson, M. T., Morgan, S. E., Roberts-Perez, S. D., Harrison, T., Afifi, W., & Long, S. D. (2008). The role of religiosity, religious norms, subjective norms, and bodily integrity in signing an organ donor card. *Health Communication, 23*, 436–447.

Talwar, V., Harris, P. L., & Schleifer, M. (Eds.). (2011). *Children's understanding of death: From biological to religious conceptions*. New York, NY: Cambridge University Press.

Thiessen, J., & Wilkins-Laflamme, S. (2017). Becoming a religious none: Irreligious socialization and disaffiliation. *Journal for the Scientific Study of Religion, 56*, 64–82.

Tsai, J. L., Koopman-Holm, B., Miyazaki, M., & Ochs, C. (2013). The religious shaping of feeling: Implications of affect valuation theory. In R. F. Paloutzian & C. L. Park (Eds.), *Handbook of the psychology of religion and spirituality* (2nd ed., pp. 274–291). New York, NY: Guilford.

Tsang, J.-A., Carlisle, R. D., & Al-Kire, R. L. (2020). Forgive and remember: The relationship between religion and the recollection of transgressions. *International Journal for the Psychology of Religion, 30*, 35–47.

Tsang, J.-A., Rowatt, W. C., & Shariff, A. (2015). Religion and prosociality. In D. A. Schroeder & W. G. Graziano (Eds.), *The Oxford handbook of prosocial behavior* (pp. 609–625). New York, NY: Oxford University Press.

Turiel, E., & Neff, K. (2000). Religion, culture, and beliefs about reality in moral reasoning. In K. S. Rosengren, C. N. Johnson, & P. L. Harris (Eds.), *Imagining the impossible: Magical, scientific, and religious thinking in children* (pp. 269–304). Cambridge, UK: Cambridge University Press.

Uzarevic, F., & Saroglou, V. (2020). Understanding nonbelievers' prejudice toward ideological opponents: The role of self-expression values and other-oriented dispositions. *International Journal for the Psychology of Religion, 30*, 161–177.

Uzarevic, F., Saroglou, V., & Muñoz-García, A. (2019). Are atheists unprejudiced? Forms of nonbelief and prejudice toward antiliberal and mainstream religious groups. *Psychology of Religion and Spirituality*. Advance online publication.

Valdesolo, P., & Graham, J. (2014). Awe, uncertainty, and agency detection. *Psychological Science, 25*, 170–178.

Van Cappellen, P., Fredrickson, B. L., Saroglou, V., & Corneille, O. (2017). Religiosity and the motivation for social affiliation. *Personality and Individual Differences, 113*, 24–31.

Van Cappellen, P., & Rimé, B. (2014). Positive emotions and self-transcendence. In V. Saroglou (Ed.), *Religion, personality, and social behavior* (pp. 123–145). New York, NY: Psychology Press.

Van Cappellen, P., Saroglou, V., Iweins, C., Piovesana, M., & Fredrickson, B. (2013). Self-transcendent positive emotions increase spirituality through basic world assumptions. *Cognition and Emotion, 27*, 1378–1394.

van der Straten Waillet, N., & Roskam, I. (2012). Religious discrimination in childhood and adolescence. *Archive for the Psychology of Religion, 34*, 215–242.

VanderWeele, T. J. (2017). Religion and health: A synthesis. In M. J. Balboni & J. R. Peteet (Eds.), *Spirituality and religion within the culture of medicine: From evidence to practice* (pp. 357–401). New York, NY: Oxford University Press.

Van Tongeren, D. R., et al. (2016). Toward an understanding of religious tolerance: Quest religiousness and positive attitudes toward religiously dissimilar others. *International Journal for the Psychology of Religion, 26*, 212–224.

Vasilenko, S. A., & Lefkowitz, E. S. (2014). Changes in religiosity after first intercourse in the transition to adulthood. *Psychology of Religion and Spirituality, 6*, 310–315.

Vishkin, A., Ben-Nun Bloom, P., & Tamir, M. (2019). Always look on the bright side of life: Religiosity, emotion regulation, and well-being in a Jewish and Christian sample. *Journal of Happiness Studies, 20*, 427–447

Vishkin, A., Bigman, Y., Porat, R., Solak, N., Halperin, E., & Tamir, M. (2016). God rest our hearts: Religiosity and cognitive reappraisal. *Emotion, 16*, 252–262.

Voas, D., McAndrew, S., & Storm, I. (2013). Modernization and the gender gap in religiosity: Evidence from cross-national European surveys. *Kölner Zeitschrift für Soziologie und Sozialpsychologie, 65*, 259–283.

Wallace, L. E., Anthony, R., End, C. M., & Way, B. M. (2019). Does religion stave off the grave? Religious affiliation in one's obituary and longevity. *Social Psychological and Personality Science, 10*, 662–670.

Watts, F. N. (2007). Emotion regulation and religion. In J. J. Gross (Ed.), *Handbook of emotion regulation* (pp. 504–520). New York, NY: Guilford.

Webster, G. D., & Duffy, R. D. (2016). Losing faith in the intelligence–religiosity link: New evidence for a decline effect, spatial dependence, and mediation by education and life quality. *Intelligence, 55*, 15–27.

Wigger, J. B. (2019). *Invisible companions: Encounters with imaginary friends, gods, ancestors, and angels.* Stanford, CA: Stanford University Press.

Willard, A. K., & Norenzayan, A. (2017). "Spiritual but not religious": Cognition, schizotypy, and conversion in understanding alternative beliefs. *Cognition, 165*, 137–146.

Willard, A. K., Shariff, A. F., & Norenzayan, A. (2016). Religious priming as a research tool for studying religion: Evidentiary value, current issues, and future directions. *Current Opinion in Psychology*, 12, 71–75.

Williams, A. D., Lau, G., & Grisham, J. R. (2013). Thought-action fusion as a mediator of religiosity and obsessive-compulsive symptoms. *Journal of Behavior Therapy and Experimental Psychiatry*, 44, 207–212.

Williams, L. M., & Lawler, M. G. (2001). Religious heterogamy and religiosity: A comparison of interchurch and same-church individuals. *Journal for the Scientific Study of Religion*, 40, 465–478.

Wilson, M. S., Bulbulia, J., & Sibley, C. G. (2014). Differences and similarities in religious and paranormal beliefs: A typology of distinct faith signatures. *Religion, Brain and Behavior*, 4, 104–126.

Wink, P., Dillon, M., & Farina, D. (2019). Religion, spirituality, and the agential self. In D. P. McAdams, R. L. Shiner, & J. L. Tacket (Eds.), *Handbook of personality development* (pp. 364–379). New York, NY: Guilford.

Woolley, J. D. (2000). The development of beliefs about direct mental-physical causality in imagination magic, and religion. In K. S. Rosengren, C. N., Johnson, & P. L. Harris (Eds.), *Imagining the impossible: Magical, scientific, and religious thinking in children* (pp. 99–129). New York, NY: Cambridge University Press.

Woolley, J. D., & Phelps, K. E. (2001). The development of children's beliefs about prayer. *Journal of Cognition and Culture*, 1, 139–166.

Wright, J. D. (2016). More religion, less justification for violence. *Archive for the Psychology of Religion*, 38, 159–183.

Wu, A., Wang, J. Y., & Jia, C. X. (2015). Religion and completed suicide: A meta-analysis. *PLoS One*, 10(6), e0131715.

Wulff, D. M. (2014). Mystical experiences. In E. Cardeña, S. J. Lynn, & S. Krippner (Eds.), *Varieties of anomalous experience: Examining the scientific evidence* (2nd ed., pp. 369–408). Washington, DC: American Psychological Association.

Yaden, D. B., Haidt, J., Hood, R. W. Jr., Vago, D. R., & Newberg, A. B. (2017). The varieties of self-transcendent experience. *Review of General Psychology*, 21, 143–160.

Yeniaras, V., & Akarsu, T. N. (2017). Religiosity and life satisfaction: A multidimensional approach. *Journal of Happiness Studies*, 18, 1815–1840.

Yeung, J. W. K. (2018). Religion, volunteerism and health: Are religious people really doing well by doing good? *Social Indicators Research*, 138, 809–828.

Yeung, J. W. K., Chan, Y., & Lee, B. K. (2009). Youth religiosity and substance use: A meta-analysis from 1995–2007. *Psychological Reports, 105,* 255–266.

Ysseldyk, R., Matheson, K., & Anisman, H. (2010). Religiosity as identity: Toward an understanding of religion from a social identity perspective. *Personality and Social Psychology Review, 14,* 60–71.

Zinnbauer, B. J., & Pargament, K. I. (2005). Religiousness and spirituality. In R. F. Paloutzian & C. L. Park (Eds.), *Handbook of the psychology of religion and spirituality* (pp. 21–42). New York, NY: Guilford.

Zuckerman, M., Silberman, J., & Hall, J. A. (2013). The relation between intelligence and religiosity: A meta-analysis and some proposed explanations. *Personality and Social Psychology Review, 17,* 325–354.

Zuckerman, P., Galen, L. W., & Pasquale, F. L. (2016). *The nonreligious: Understanding secular people and societies.* New York, NY: Oxford University Press.

Zukerman, G., & Korn, L. (2014). Post-traumatic stress and world assumptions: The effects of religious coping. *Journal of Religion and Health, 53,* 1676–1690.